TALES OF OHIO'S
UNDERGROUND
RAILROAD

TALES OF OHIO'S
UNDERGROUND
RAILROAD

DAVID MEYERS
and
ELISE MEYERS WALKER

THE
History
PRESS

Published by The History Press
Charleston, SC
www.historypress.com

Front cover: "The Underground Railroad," by Charles T. Webber, 1897. *Courtesy National Underground Railroad Freedom Center/Wikimedia Commons. Back cover*: Eliza from George Peck's production of *Uncle Tom's Cabin. Courtesy Library of Congress.*

First published 2025

Manufactured in the United States

ISBN 9781467159166

Library of Congress Control Number: 2024949767

Notice: The information in this book is true and complete to the best of our knowledge. It is offered without guarantee on the part of the author or The History Press. The author and The History Press disclaim all liability in connection with the use of this book.

To the legions of dedicated Ohio historians, especially my friends Randy McNutt and Cheryl Bauer.
They have made my life richer by their friendship and their books.

CONTENTS

ACKNOWLEDGEMENTS

I have been writing books for Arcadia Publishing/The History Press since 2008. During that period, I have worked with numerous people in the organization without having met any of them. Yet, I feel I have developed some friendships. Occasionally, I have expressed my gratitude to them for the help they have given me, but not often enough. So, accept this as a belated thank you to those who I should have thanked before this, especially John Rodrigue, Joe Gartrell, Katie Perry, Emily Lamont, Zoe Ames and others whose names escape me.

THE UPPERGROUND RAILROAD

The dictates of humanity came in opposition to the law of the land,
and we ignored the law.
—Levi Coffin[1]

By the time Ohio became a state in 1803, there were already forces at work seeking to free the nation's slaves. What to do about slavery had been part of the ongoing political debate ever since the Articles of Confederation were drafted. However, it had to be put on the back burner in the interest of getting the new country up and running. States' rights—including the right to own slaves—had to be honored, or there would be no United States.

But many of the enslaved took it upon themselves to run away from their masters in the quest for freedom. Nearly all who reached the Ohio River or the Mason-Dixon Line did so by their own devices. Initially, they had little help. Over time, however, some found people of good conscience—both Black and White—who would willingly violate the law to assist them in their escape. As a result of such individual actions, a network of sorts arose more or less organically, which came to be called the Underground Railroad.

In his autobiography, abolitionist Frederick Douglass wrote that he had "never approved of the very public manner in which some of our western friends have conducted what they call the *underground railroad*, but which, I think, by their open declarations, has been made most emphatically the *upperground* railroad."[2] And by "western friends" he primarily meant the abolitionists of Ohio—the hotbed of Underground Railroad activity.

Douglass—a fugitive from slavery himself—was concerned that the abolitionists were drawing too much attention to their work, which would prompt slave owners to increase their vigilance. "I would keep the merciless slaveholder profoundly ignorant of the means of flight adopted by the slave," Douglass declared. "I would leave him to imagine himself surrounded by myriads of invisible tormentors, ever ready to snatch from his infernal grasp his trembling prey."[3]

When the *Narrative of the Life of Frederick Douglass* was first published in 1845, the Underground Railroad (or UGRR) was still in its infancy. Although the enslaved had been fleeing from their owners since time immemorial, the informal network of people that would come to be called the UGRR appeared during the early years of the nineteenth century. And, to Douglass's point, much of what we know about it is due to the publicity it received.

While Douglass felt this was detrimental to its purpose, he did not know how the story would end. However, by having "outed" himself as a fugitive, Douglass risked being arrested and returned to slavery at any time. So he fled to Great Britain and did not return to the United States until nineteen months later, after his British supporters purchased his freedom.[4]

In an earlier book, *The Reverse Underground Railroad in Ohio*, we discussed how the laws governing fugitive slaves—or, more accurately, enslaved persons, a term that reflects their circumstance and not their essence—gradually evolved from the birth of our nation through the end of the Civil War. Our purpose was to highlight the struggle that was taking place in all branches of government, federal and state, as public sentiment on the issue of slavery shifted. And it was the "problem" of the enslaved versus slaveholders' rights that was driving the debate.

Although Ohio was a Free State from its inception, many slaves could be found within its borders until the mid-1830s—and not just runaways. Author Rufus King, a signer of the U.S. Constitution, noted,

> There had been a certain tacit tolerance of slavery by the people of the state, so that Southern slave owners visiting Ohio, or traveling through, were accompanied by their servants, without question, and by a sort of common concession of right. Numbers of slaves as many as two thousand it was sometimes supposed, were hired in southern Ohio from Virginia and Kentucky, chiefly by farmers.[5]

But by 1840, there had been a sea change. The abolitionist movement was gaining momentum, and a handful of its most prominent leaders started

Abolitionist Frederick Douglass lamented that the Underground Railroad had become an "upperground railroad." *Courtesy of Library of Congress.*

taking legal action to secure the freedom of enslaved visitors to Ohio. Others went even further and began enticing slaves to make a dash for freedom. A nascent Underground Railroad was developing through the efforts of various alliances of people—both Black and White—working independently.

In *Tales of Ohio's Underground Railroad*, we have brought together many more compelling stories about these brave men and women who endeavored to help fugitive slaves, often risking their own lives and freedom.[6] Throughout these stories, the whole array of attitudes toward slavery are on display. It wasn't just a matter of being for or against. There were many positions between those two points that show how different groups attempted to come to terms with their own conflicted feelings on the issue. For example, many of the founding fathers couldn't bring themselves to free their own slaves even as they espoused views in opposition to slavery. They either couldn't afford or were unwilling to make the personal sacrifice to do so.

At a time when British policymakers were considering throwing their support behind the Confederacy during the Civil War, English economist John Elliot Cairnes made the following observation:

> *The system of slavery might be, perhaps, upheld logically if the negro race could be proved to be not men, but a kind of monkey race made to wait on men. But facts are too strong, and the Southern upholders of slavery have never attempted to prove that; what they do say is, that the negroes are inferior and cannot govern themselves; that slavery is a "divine institution" for civilizing and Christianizing these savage African races. As regards the alleged inferiority, I am convinced the negro is superior in some qualities, and how far inferior in others cannot be asserted until he and the white man are placed in exactly the same position. Where they have been, the negro has not acquitted himself discreditably.[7]*

With so many fascinating UGRR stories to be told, it's puzzling that people feel the need to propagate unconfirmed legends or outright lies. But they do. And these myths, mendacities and, occasionally, honest mistakes concerning the UGRR survive and prosper, despite efforts to dispel them. What's worse, they have served to distort and displace the true history of this remarkable undertaking. Consequently, we have addressed one of these major topics at the beginning of each chapter.

Comparatively few persons held in slavery actually escaped, and most were soon recaptured. But frequent newspaper accounts of runaway slaves kept the issue in the public consciousness and fostered growing unrest in the South. Then, when Confederate forces bombarded the Union soldiers at Fort Sumter, South Carolina, on April 12, 1861, the war between the North and the South commenced, and the flow of runaway slaves into Ohio virtually stopped. The era of the UGRR was at an end.

Although Levi Coffin, William Still, William Mitchell, Harriett Tubman and a few other key figures would write about their involvement, it wasn't

Left: Confederate commander John Singleton Mosby admitted he had committed treason and was proud of it. *Courtesy of Library of Congress.*

Right: After the war, Colonel Mosby threw his support behind General Ulysses S. Grant (pictured) for president. *Courtesy of Library of Congress.*

until Wilbur H. Siebert, a professor of history at Ohio State University, began systematically collecting information on the UGRR through letters and interviews that people began to appreciate the full extent of this loosely connected enterprise. In her assessment of Wilbur Siebert's flawed yet indispensable study, Kathryn Schulz—an expert on human error—wrote, "That story, like so many that we tell about our nation's past, has a tricky relationship to the truth: not quite wrong, but simplified; not quite a myth, but mythologized."[8]

Contemporaneous with Siebert, a movement that would come to be called the Lost Cause was underway, which gloried in the supposed virtues of the antebellum South. Its adherents dismissed the role of slavery as the reason for the "War Between the States" or the "War of Northern Aggression" (their preferred term) and argued that Southerners were simply defending their way of life against Yankee interference—a way of life that included the institution of slavery.

Confederate Colonel John Singleton Mosby, however, scoffed at those who claimed the war was fought over the southern states' right to secede from the Union. "I always understood we went to War on account of the thing we quarreled with the North about," Mosby said. "I never heard of any other cause of quarrel than slavery."[9] Mosby had no patience for those who espoused the mythology of the "Lost Cause." He shunned reunions, thought statues were a waste of money and refused to join large veterans' organizations. He also objected to the near-deification of General Robert E. Lee as a great military leader.

"Men fight from sentiment," Mosby later wrote. "After the fight is over they invent some fanciful theory on which they imagine that they fought."[10] Known as the Gray Ghost for his celebrated exploits as a guerrilla cavalry leader, Mosby never apologized for his actions: "I committed treason and I am proud of it."[11] But after the war, Mosby became a Republican and aligned himself with President Ulysses S. Grant, thereby removing himself from the pantheon of Confederate war heroes. As he once wrote to a friend, "There was more vindictiveness shown to me by the Virginia people for my voting for Grant than the North showed to me for fighting four years against him."[12]

But history is not what happened; it's what was recorded. That is its failing. It's also why the propagandists of the Lost Cause set out to control

The Robert E. Lee statue in New Orleans was one of many Confederate memorials taken down in the early twenty-first century. *Courtesy Abdazizar/Wikipedia.*

the narrative, most visibly by erecting hundreds of Confederate statues and memorials throughout the United States—more than thirty since the beginning of the twenty-first century alone. Such politicization of public monuments remains an ongoing threat to our interpretation of history.

Yet every historian dips into the same reservoir of facts, and all that separates them is their interpretation of those facts. Roughly 175 years after the UGRR came to an end, there is little likelihood that any new information remains to be discovered. Although many thousands of slaves may have escaped from captivity, we know only the stories of those that were written down. It is from these that we make observations and draw conclusions. And for the most part, we have allowed the stories to speak for themselves in our previous book and in this one.

David Meyers

Chapter 1

WALKING PROPERTY WALKED OFF

Before there was an Underground Railroad, there was an underground railroad. They just didn't call it that. But whatever they did call this system for aiding fugitives from slavery in their escape to freedom, it apparently didn't catch on. Still, they must have called it something during their secret planning meetings.

Ohio abolitionist Rush R. Sloane believed that the metaphorical title Underground Railroad was inspired by the story of Tice Davids. Sometime in 1831, Davids came to Sandusky and tarried a while before heading on to Canada. As Sloane recounted more than fifty years later:

> *When he was running away his master, a Kentuckian, was in close pursuit and pressing him so hard that when the Ohio river was reached he had no alternative but to jump in and swim across. It took his master some time to secure a skiff in which he and his aid followed the swimming fugitive, keeping him in sight until he had landed. Once on shore, however, he could not find him. No one had seen him. And after a long and unsuccessful search the disappointed slave-master went into Ripley, and when inquired of as to what had become of his slave, said he could not tell; that he had searched all the openings, but he could not find him; that he was close behind him when the boy got on shore, and he thought "the nigger must have gone off on an underground road."*[13]

So presumably somebody in Ripley heard the story, told somebody else and it spread from there. Note that Sloane did not use the phrase *underground railroad*, and for good reason. The first railroad in Kentucky was chartered the year before Davids made his escape. At the time, there was just twenty-three miles of railroad operating in the entire country. So it is unlikely that anyone would have been thinking in terms of a railroad, underground or otherwise. Kentucky's first railroad, the Lexington & Ohio, didn't break ground until October 1831, and the mile and a half of track didn't open until the following year.

Eight years later, in the October 11, 1839 edition of the Boston *Liberator*, a leading abolitionist newspaper, Hiram Wilson of Toronto, who performed missionary work among the runaways, called for the creation of "a great republican railroad…constructed from Mason and Dixon's to the Canada line, upon which fugitives from slavery might come pouring into this province."[14] As "railway mania" was starting to roll out across the United States, perhaps Wilson's suggestion caught the fancy of other opponents of slavery—sort of a mash-up of "underground road" with "republican railroad." Or maybe it was just a coincidence.

However, it now appears that the first published usage of the expression was in the August 10, 1842 *Tocsin of Liberty*, an abolitionist newspaper published in Albany, New York. According to biographer Scott Shane, Thomas Smallwood, who had himself been born into slavery and bought his freedom only eleven days earlier, contributed a satirical piece to the newspaper about a conversation he had with a Washington slaveholder whose "walking property walked off," as he put it.[15] In response, Smallwood told the man "that it was your cruelty to him, that made him disappear by that same 'under ground rail-road' or 'steam balloon,' about which one of your city constables was swearing so bitterly a few weeks ago, when complaining that the 'd—d rascals' got off so, and that no trace of them could be found!"[16]

Smallwood later attributed the remark to John Zell, a Baltimore police officer who regularly collected rewards from slave owners in exchange for returning their runaways to them. So it was Constable Zell, son of a Pennsylvania slaveholder and no friend of the Black man, who most likely first referred to an underground railroad, if only in an angry rant.[17]

A month or so later, the *Tocsin* ran the following news item, which likely fixed the concept in the public imagination: "Twenty six Slaves in one Week—Sam Weller is requested to tell the slave-holders that we passed twenty-six prime slaves to the land of freedom last week, and several more

403 Adams Street was the home of well-known Sandusky abolitionist Rush R. Sloan.
Courtesy Nyttend/Wikipedia.

this week thus far. Don't know what the end of the week will foot up. All went by 'the underground railroad.'"[18]

The newspaper's new editor, Massachusetts abolitionist Charles T. Torrey, not only embraced the name but also organized his own Underground Railroad route from Washington, D.C., to Albany, New York, and ultimately Canada, working in collaboration with Smallwood.[19] And within a year or

The Liberty Bell in Philadelphia's Independence Hall was the original "Tocsin of Liberty." *Courtesy of Library of Congress.*

two, the term began to take root. Although some newspapers belittled the UGRR's ineffectiveness, the *Green-Mountain Freeman* charged in 1844 that the Whig Party under Henry Clay had "provided an *armed patrol* for the city of Washington, at the expense of the nation, to execute the monstrous police laws of that city, and watch the slaves lest they should get to the underground railroad."[20] Clearly, somebody thought the UGRR was having an impact.

Ohio newspapers such as the *Portage Sentinel* and *Anti-Slavery Bugle* started using the term as early as 1845, although Underground Railroad activities in the Buckeye State were already well underway. But depending on a person's geographical location, they might have doubted the very existence of the UGRR itself. As Elias S. Gilbert of Ontario County, New York, confided in a letter to E.C. Wixom in 1902, "I do not believe there was any such organized Under Ground Rail Road as many suppose. That is a myth. The facts are that slaves got away and were helped in about as many ways as there were individuals to go or men to help them."[21] And Gilbert was one of the helpers.

In a way, Gilbert wasn't wrong. This was the position historian Larry Gara took in his book *The Liberty Line*, challenging the whole notion of the

Yours for the slave
Charles T. Torrey

Charles Turner Torrey organized his own UGRR from Washington, D.C., to Albany, New York. *Courtesy Wikipedia.*

Underground Railroad. As Gara pointed out, "In many cases it was the slaves themselves who took things into their own hands, planned their escapes, and during the greater part of their journeys arranged for or managed their own transportation, without the assistance of the legendary underground railroad."[22] True enough, but Gara seems to have been as guilty of cherry-picking data as those he was criticizing.[23] Some escapes were solitary endeavors and others were undertaken with assistance, but most were not documented in any fashion.

In truth, the Underground Railroad sprang up fairly spontaneously in many different places (northern places, that is, although there were a few helpers in the South) at much the same time as the need for it was recognized. And like success, the UGRR had many fathers, as well as a number of mothers, only a small number of whom ever received credit due to the secretive nature of the system.

Slave owners often found it difficult to understand why their bond servants (a politer term for *slave*) would run away. After all, they believed that by its very nature, slavery as a system was as beneficial for the slave as it was for the enslaver. Some of them even insisted that their slaves were so happy in their condition that they would never think to leave it unless they were enticed to do so by some evil abolitionist. Of course, this was based on the presumption—supported by "science"—that people of color were a lower form of life in God's creation. In the nineteenth century, Harvard Professor Louis Agassiz, for example, argued that White people were biologically superior to Black people—or any other race, for that matter.

Yet Ona Maria Judge, a slave who served as a maid to Martha Washington, wife of President George Washington, decided to run away early in 1797. A "light mulatto girl, much freckled" and "almost white," Ona had been living in the president's house in Philadelphia.[24] However, on learning she was going to be sent back to his plantation in Virginia, she slipped away and was never caught. Years later, she gave an interview to the *Granite Freeman*, a New Hampshire newspaper, in which she explained she simply wanted to be free. And she wasn't the only one.

What might be Ohio's earliest fugitive slave story was pieced together by historian Henry Robert Burke. It concerns a young African American man who was held in bondage by the pioneering Tomlinson family. One Tomlinson son, Joseph II (or Junior), had settled downriver from Wheeling, (West) Virginia, in 1770, while his father, Joseph I (Senior), and a brother, Samuel, established a "tomahawk claim" at Williams Station (later Williamstown) even farther down the Ohio, opposite the mouth of the Muskingum River.[25] They brought a number of slaves with them.

Junior worked the slaves at both the Flats of Grave Creek, just below Moundsville, and Williams Station. According to Burke, two slaves, one of whom was named Mike, ran away from Williams Station one day in 1804. "They crossed the Ohio River at Marietta," Burke related, "and traveled about 35 miles north on the Muskingum to Owl Creek, where they stopped at a farm owned by William Craig."[26] Although this was before the Underground Railroad had commenced, Craig's first impulse was to help the two men.

When they learned the whereabouts of the fugitives, Junior Tomlinson, his son Robert and several others set out to recapture them. Robert and Mike had grown up together and had been "friends," to the extent a slave and his master's son can be. But not anymore. As the slave hunters drew near, they were spotted by Craig, who alerted the runaways.

"The two slaves started running," Burke wrote, "but Robert was very swift of foot and soon overtook Mike and knocked him to the ground, using his rifle as a club."[27] Mike was clobbered several more times before he pulled a knife and stabbed Robert, who cried out for his father before dying. While his companion managed to escape, Mike was immediately apprehended.

"After burying his son, [Junior] started across country with Mike, headed for Grave Creek."[28] That night, the party camped at Negro Run, six miles west of Cumberland in Guernsey County. While there, they met two men, Reeve and Cochran, who were traveling to Kentucky. Surprisingly, perhaps, the men later reported to the authorities in Muskingum County, Ohio, that they saw Junior execute Mike at Negro Run. Apparently, these two White men were troubled by the treatment accorded the Black man. Following a coroner's inquest at Putnam, Governor Edward Tiffin of Ohio asked the Virginia attorney general to extradite Joseph Tomlinson Jr., but he refused. For many years afterward, Mike's unburied bones lay scattered at the murder site.

Not long after Ohio became a state in 1803, Jane Smith and her husband, Reverend William Williamson, arrived from North Carolina, accompanied by their twenty-seven slaves. Having come to believe that slavery was evil, the Williamsons were determined to set them free. However, the former slaves would have had to leave the state within six months if the Williamsons had emancipated them in North Carolina. So, like a number of other slave owners did, they chose to do so once they reached Ohio.[29]

Perhaps a dozen or so years later, the Williamsons received a visit from John Smith, Jane's brother. Traveling with him was an enslaved man. Named Joseph Logan or Joseph Smith, he was better known as Black Joe. Having been born in bondage, Joe first acquired some knowledge of what it meant to live in a Free State during his brief sojourn in Ohio.

About 1817, Joe "contracted a slave marriage with Jemima, a black girl of about seventeen years of age, the property of another branch of the Smith family."[30] When Jemima's owner died two years later, the Williamsons' daughter, Jane Smith Williamson, received a "legacy" of $300.[31] Normally, this would have been paid through the sale of slaves, but Jane would not permit it. Instead, she agreed to take Jemima and her children to satisfy the inheritance and then emancipate them.

When Jane went to North Carolina to claim the slaves, Joe begged her to buy him as well, but she did not have the means to do so. Then, on March 10, 1821, Jane, her brother Thomas, Jemima and one child (the other having died during the interim) began their return trip to Ohio on horseback.

That summer, Joe's owner took him to Ohio to visit the Williamsons, and Joe was allowed to spend some time with his wife. Although his master promised he would eventually give him his freedom, Joe did not intend to wait. On their return trip to North Carolina, he memorized the route, made friends with any slaves he met along the way and "privately beat and whipped all the slave-hunting dogs in the vicinity of his home, so that they would refuse to follow him."[32]

The following summer, Joe struck out for Ohio on his own. Although his owner would not pursue him, knowing he would never permit himself to be taken alive, professional slave catchers did. But Joe killed any dogs that dared follow him. On reaching the Poage settlement in Tennessee, he "learned that Colonel James Poage had taken his slaves north and set them free" in the vicinity of Ripley, Ohio.[33] When he finally came to the Ohio River near Ashland, Kentucky, Joe swam across and then started west.

By now, Joe felt it was safe to travel during the day. But not far from Portsmouth, he encountered two slave hunters. After he picked one of them up and tossed him over a fence, the other decided not to try to tangle with him. A stonecutter near Bentonville also thought about trying to capture him, but Joe scared him away by threatening to kill him.

An 1820 print of the fabled steamboat *Walk-in-the-Water. Courtesy of Library of Congress.*

The following day, Joe arrived at the Beeches, the Williamsons' place in Adams County. The first person to see him was Jemima. Although Joe's master was tipped off about where he was, he refused to provide a reward to the slave hunters who offered their services, knowing that the fugitive would not be taken alive. Joe subsequently settled into a new life in southern Ohio, where he became a prominent member of the Underground Railroad, brazenly assisting other runaway slaves like himself.

By Rush Sloane's recollection, the first freedom seeker came to Sandusky, Ohio, in the fall of 1820. He arrived alone and on foot. Somehow, he found his way to the home of Abner Strong on Strong's Ridge in Huron County. Believing it would not be safe for the Black man to remain at his house, Strong took him to Captain P. Shephard, who was living in a tavern kept by C.W. Marsh. Shephard hid the runaway in the tavern's barn. He was aided by John, an African American hostler who tended the horses. Such cooperative efforts were the foundation for what was becoming the Underground Railroad.

On the same day the fugitive arrived in Sandusky, his owner did as well. John Riley had been pursuing him across the state on horseback and had tracked him as far as Strong's place. "For three days the master, aided by Captain Shephard, waited, searched and watched," Sloane recalled.[34] Riley even offered Shephard $300 in gold if he located the slave, little suspecting that he was in league with him.

Unable to find the slave after four days, Riley took the steamboat *Walk-in-the-Water* to Detroit. Captain Shephard then loaded the fugitive on his own small sailboat and landed him in Malden, Canada, before the end of the next day. He was believed to have been the first fugitive from slavery to reach Canada by way of Sandusky. Not long afterward, Riley, the slave owner, returned to Sandusky, settled up his account at the tavern and headed for home empty-handed.

Chapter 2

THIS LITTLE LIGHT OF MINE

The Rankin House, sitting atop a three-hundred-foot bluff overlooking the Ohio River, is one of the best-documented Underground Railroad stations to be found anywhere. And it is generally accepted that the Reverend John C. Rankin placed a candle or a lantern in the window of his home—or possibly suspended the lantern from a thirty-foot flagpole in his front yard—as a signal to fugitives from slavery on the Kentucky side that help awaited them. They just had to make their way across the river somehow.

As John Parker, a former slave himself who lived below in the town of Ripley, told journalist Frank Gregg, "A lighted candle stood as a beacon which could be seen from across the river, and like the North Star was the guide to the fleeing slave."[35] Although no actual research has been done with candles, scientists have estimated, based on astronomical studies, that an unaided human eye could see a candle flame at one and a half miles under optimal conditions. But the view from Kentucky to Rankin's house was sometimes less than optimal due to physical obstructions, thickness of the atmosphere, weather conditions and other factors.

So did other agents of the Underground Railroad use similar signals? Again, Parker related that at the homes of many Ripley abolitionists, including himself, "the door was always ajar, and the candle in the room lighted and waiting to welcome any and all who entered."[36] Robert E. Fee in Moscow, Ohio, twenty-five miles downriver, purportedly kept a light in his window as well. While it's an attractive image, it doesn't explain how

The view across the Ohio River from the Rankin house in Ripley. *Courtesy Kevin Myers/Wikipedia.*

The Rankin House just above Ripley, prior to restoration. *Courtesy of Library of Congress.*

the fugitives differentiated the safe houses from the unsafe ones, since all presumably burned candles or lamps to some extent.

Besides candles and lanterns, other signals were supposedly used by the UGRR. In a 1903 pamphlet, Elijah Huftelen discussed the use of a "dead bush":

> *Nothing was more common along highways than an occasional dead bush and its use as a signal would easily escape the notice of anyone not looking for it. No matter how long the road might seem no turn was to be made until a signal was reached. These signals were never disturbed except to be renewed if they had decayed or if not firmly fixed had blown away.*[37]

Huftelen, who had purportedly helped a stationmaster in LeRoy, New York, as a young boy, also indicated that these signals were used to identify safe houses. However, who would have created these signals and then maintained them is not addressed. Neither is how to distinguish a dead bush used as a signal from an ordinary dead bush, not to mention any suggestion of how this "code" was disseminated among those residents of slave states who were being held in bondage. While the UGRR may have used some kind of signals, the surviving literature is generally silent about such matters.

Isaac Brandt, who said he knew John Brown in Lawrence County, Iowa, recalled a meeting they once had while Brown was transporting fugitives. "I saw that he had a load in his wagon and gave him the signal for safety and he understood."[38] Although he did not explain what that signal was, Brandt went on to ask, "How did Brown know I could be trusted?" before answering his own question.[39]

> *Well, even if he had not met me before he knew it when I said "hello," much as we do now at the telephone. That was a pretty much well established underground railroad signal for all's well. In response he lifted his right hand to his ear and grasped the rim firmly between thumb and finger. That meant he understood. If he had held up his hand with the palm extended outward, it would have been different.*[40]

Brandt admitted he did not know how the signs or signals were developed but claimed that without them, the operation of the UGRR would not have been possible.

At the former Depp Settlement in Delaware County, Ohio, a bell is on display that was purportedly used to signal to fugitive slaves that all was clear, presumably after slave hunters had left the area.[41] But this would have been known only to those who had already sought refuge in this historic Black community. The important question to ask whenever someone suggests that a white-painted chimney with a black top or colored ribbons tied to tree limbs or various hand signs were a code used to communicate with fugitives from slavery is this: How would they have learned the code?

According to Kate Clifford Larson, author of *Bound for the Promised Land*, a biography of Harriet Tubman, the former slave and UGRR conductor used bird calls when she was leading fugitives from slavery to freedom. "We know that she used the call of any owl to alert refugees and her freedom seekers that it was OK, or not OK, to come out of hiding and continue their journey," Angela Crenshaw, a ranger at Harriet Tubman Underground Railroad State Park in Church Creek, Maryland, explained in *Audubon Magazine*. "It would have been the Barred Owl, or at it is sometimes called, a 'hoot-owl.'"[42]

However, like nearly all signals mentioned in slave narratives, this was an impromptu arrangement, created on the spur of the moment for a specific situation, rather than a sophisticated system of codes developed by some centralized UGRR body—because there wasn't one. Harriet always did things her own way. For example, her biblical reference in an 1854 letter alerted her brothers of her intent to rescue them: "When the good old ship of Zion comes along…be ready to step aboard."[43] No one else would have understood her meaning.

In September 1823, an unnamed Black couple and their two children were passing through Bloomfield, Trumbull County, Ohio, while on the way to Ashtabula, a popular departure point for Canada.[44] They had purportedly escaped from their master in Virginia, and apparently, they were unaccompanied. Unbeknownst to them, a party of three slave catchers from Virginia, possibly including the owner and his son, arrived at a nearby tavern a few hours later, as darkness was approaching. Worn out from their travels, the trio elected to stay the night, after gaining the assurance of the innkeeper that he would wake them at an early hour.

Soon the townspeople were abuzz with the news that there were slave catchers among them. Squire Ephraim Brown, an abolitionist and Underground Railroad conductor in spirit if not in fact, set out in his wagon with a band of men to find and hide the slaves, who were located at a house near Rome. At first, the owner was suspicious of their motives and prepared to repel them. But once they convinced him they were there to help, he assisted them in moving the fugitive family to a barn that stood far off the road.

All the while, the Virginians were blissfully asleep. Instead of waking them as requested, the innkeeper instructed everyone else in the tavern to be as quiet as possible the next morning. When the men finally awoke, they found that "a singular torpor seemed to come over every one about that tavern on that night, so that it was late in the morning before any one was aroused; the breakfast was delayed, the key of the stable lock could not be found, and when at last the stable was opened, the Virginian horses were each found to have cast a shoe."[45] Such passive-aggressive behavior was not unusual among abolitionists, especially the pacifist Quakers.

The slave catchers then had difficulty locating the blacksmith. When they finally did, he didn't have any nails and had to make new shoes. But by then, his fire had gone out, so he was unable to shoe the horses until nearly noon. Only then could the Virginians set out on their quest. Along the way, the three men passed the barn in southern Ashtabula County where the fugitive family was hiding. As soon as the hunters were out of sight, the fugitives were taken back to Bloomfield and hidden away in a rude hut in a deep wood.

Three days later, the Virginians returned to the tavern. This time, they found a warrant that had been issued by Squire Kimble, charging them with running the tollgate on the turnpike just north of Warren. According to historian Henry Howe, "On passing the gate they had supposed that the objects of their pursuit had taken the State road toward Painesville, and therefore paid the half toll necessary to go by that route; whereas, if they had represented that they were coming to Bloomfield, they would have been required to pay full toll."[46]

Turned away from the stable, the slave hunters tied their horses to a signpost and then went to see Squire Kimble, who fined them five dollars apiece and costs. Returning to their horses, they found that the manes and tails of each animal had been shorn and a note had been attached to one of the saddles. It read:

> *Slave-hunters, beware!*
> *For sincerely we swear*
> *That if again here*
> *You ever appear,*
> *We'll give you the coat of a Tory to wear.*[47]

Meanwhile, the fugitives lingered in Bloomfield for some time while the father worked for Squire Brown. Eventually, they continued on their journey to freedom aboard a Canada-bound vessel, their fares paid by their new friends.

Elisha Young was a fugitive slave from Kentucky who made his way to Alum Creek Settlement, a Quaker community in Marengo, Morrow County, Ohio. He soon went to work for a man named Aaron Benedict, helping him with his farm. As a precaution, he changed his name to John Green. Although he was treated well, Young was not a happy man because his wife and two children were still being held in bondage. So he resolved to rescue them with Benedict's assistance.

Early in the autumn of 1837, the two men hitched a team of horses to a carriage and began making their way to Ripley, often traveling under the cover of darkness. At Ripley, they called on Reverend John Rankin, one of the most respected abolitionists on the Ohio River. A Presbyterian minister from Tennessee, Rankin had moved his family to Ripley, Ohio, on New Year's Eve 1821 after learning that a like-minded contingent of Virginians had settled there. Rankin found that a band of abolitionists was already engaged in aiding fugitive slaves in their escape to freedom, and he would soon become one of its prominent leaders.

After Rankin rowed Young across to Kentucky at night, he told Young to burn a signal light at a designated spot when he was ready to return to Ohio. "About a fortnight later, [Young] returned, with his family from a sixty-mile trip into Kentucky, and made his signal as agreed upon."[48] Rankin and Benedict took the rowboat across to the Kentucky shore to pick them up.

The next night, Benedict, Young and the rest of their party began driving north on their return journey to Morrow County. Once again, they mostly traveled at night and stayed with friends during the day. At last, they reached Marengo, where Young and his family lived in a cabin not far from the home of Benedict, their benefactor.

A month and a half later, a band of men came to Young's cabin one night when he was away, having made the trip from Delaware. Entering the house, they grabbed his wife and children from their beds and hurried off with them. Young, who was hunting for raccoon in a nearby wood with Aaron's cousin Mordecai Benedict heard someone blowing the alarm horn. The men emerged from the woods just in time to see the wagon being rapidly driven away.

As soon as they were able, Young and Mordecai set off after them on horseback. They first sought a warrant but were delayed when they couldn't locate the sheriff. Finally, they enlisted the help of a constable from Bellepoint on the Scioto River. By then, the kidnappers had fled toward West Jefferson on the National Road. The men gave chase and overtook them as they were drinking in a tavern, fourteen miles outside of Columbus. However, the "constable would neither serve the warrant nor surrender it."[49] There was nothing Young and Mordecai could do except return home.

Sensing that it would be unsafe for him to remain in Marengo, Young headed for Canada on the Underground Railroad. He learned later that his wife died two years after she was captured. Following the Civil War, Young returned to Ohio, where he lived for a while in Ashley. He then went to Kentucky, found his daughter and brought her and her husband back with him. They then settled in Van Wert County.

In a purported confession made to her kidnappers, Eliza Jane said she was born a slave in New Orleans. In 1834, she escaped to Cincinnati aboard the *Tuscarora*, a packet ship plying the Mississippi. She then made her way to Ripley, Ohio, where she married Gabriel Johnson and gave birth to five children. Although a Black woman, she also joined the Ripley Anti-Slavery Society. Not all such organizations were integrated.

On September 22, 1837, James Fox and a number of men from Kentucky abducted Eliza Jane from her home, "without warrant or shadow of authority of any kind."[50] She was taken to Mason County, Kentucky, and locked in a dirt-floored cell. According to historian Stephen Middleton, "Johnson was victim to a conspiracy concocted by Arthur Fox, of Kentucky, who instructed his son to seize a servant for the family."[51]

One of the most iconic images in *Uncle Tom's Cabin* is that of Eliza Harris crossing the frozen Ohio River. *Courtesy of Library of Congress.*

Fox, Eliza Jane's purported owner and also the county sheriff, finally admitted that his son and his agents had taken her "by mistake," but she was not released. The same gang that had kidnapped her now claimed "she had acknowledged herself to be the slave of a Mr. Johns, of New Orleans, one thousand miles further from her home."[52] Although members of the Ripley Anti-Slavery Society protested her unlawful incarceration, Judge Walker Reid refused to give her up.

Finally, on March 12, 1838, the Ohio Anti-Slavery Society secured her release through the intervention of Ohio Governor Joseph Vance.

Reverend William M. Mitchell (pictured) said that Eliza Harris's real name was Mary. *Courtesy Wikipedia.*

There would be many such tug-of-wars between the Ohio and Kentucky governors. A rumor soon gained traction that U.S. Senator Thomas Morris, during a visit to Ripley, had said "that war ought to be immediately declared against Kentucky; that perfect non-intercourse should take place, and that every Kentuckian should be shot down as soon as he set foot on the Ohio side"—strong words from a Democrat.[53]

The character of Eliza Harris in *Uncle Tom's Cabin* was believed to have been inspired by a story John Rankin told Calvin Stowe, a professor at Lane Theological Seminary. Stowe was the husband of Harriett Beecher Stowe, the book's author. According to Rankin, Eliza Harris was a young slave woman who escaped across the frozen Ohio River to the town of Ripley in February 1838, carrying a child in her arms. She then stayed at Rankin's home before making her way farther north. However, efforts to uncover the real Eliza Harris have been unsuccessful.

To begin with, Eliza Harris was not her real name but a pseudonym created by Levi Coffin to conceal her identity. Reverend William M. Mitchell wrote that the girl told him her name was Mary. According to Coffin, Eliza's master lived across the Ohio River from Ripley. Her master and mistress purportedly did not mistreat her. But when they experienced financial difficulties, they decided they would have to auction her off. Fearing she would be separated from her child, Eliza made up her mind to escape. So one night, she began walking toward the Ohio River, carrying her child in her arms. Reaching the river near daybreak, she saw that it was clogged with large blocks of floating ice. At first, she sought shelter with a kindly family, but as evening approached, she saw a band of slave catchers closing in on her.

In desperation, Eliza started across the river, springing from one floating cake of ice to another. "No fear or thought of personal danger entered Eliza's mind, for she felt that she had rather be drowned than to be captured and separated from her child."[54] By the time she reached the opposite shore, she was wet to the waist and half-frozen.

Fortunately, a man had been watching her cross and immediately gave her assistance. She was directed to the house of John Rankin, on a hill overlooking Ripley. The Rankins cared for her for several days and then forwarded her to the home of Levi Coffin in Newport, Indiana, where she was also put up for several days before continuing on to Canada.

"From the fact that Eliza Harris was sheltered at our house several days," Coffin related, "it was generally believed among those acquainted with the circumstances that I and my wife were the veritable Simeon and Rachel Halliday, the Quaker couple alluded to in 'Uncle Tom's Cabin.'"[55] However, like many of the characters in the novel, Eliza was likely a composite of several people.

Chapter 3

IT TOOK A VILLAGE

T he Putnam Historic District is a reminder that the present city of Zanesville began as a sharply divided community. Originally named Springfield, Putnam lies just west across the Muskingum River from Zanesville proper, between the Pennsylvania Railroad and Van Buren Street. Think of this body of water as their own Ohio River or Mason–Dixon Line, except it runs north and south.

The district's most notable landmark is the Stone Academy. Built in 1809 by Dr. Increase Mathews, Levi Whipple and Ebenezer Buckingham, the Stone Academy was Putnam's bid to replace Chillicothe as the state capitol. However, the town lost out to John McIntire and his Zanesville friends, who constructed their own building that served as the capital, though for only two years.

The Stone Academy, however, did not go to waste. Since Putnam was already a hotbed of abolitionism, the Stone Academy would host two conventions of the Ohio Abolition Society, in 1835 and 1839. According to local historian Norris F. Schneider,

> *Putnamites were Abolitionists. Zanesvillians, mostly from the South, were pro-slavery. Once Zanesville people formed a mob and started across the old covered Third Street Bridge to burn Abolitionist Putnam to the ground. Putnam men met them at the end of the bridge. Rich Zanesville men pulled out gold watches and pocket books and offered them to the Zanesville rowdies if they would shoot. But the sheriff arrived in time to prevent bloodshed.*[56]

The most prominent abolitionists were the Guthrie brothers (George, Stephen and Austin), the Buckinghams and the Sturgeses. The families were all related by marriage. While there seems to be little doubt that they and others were active in the Underground Railroad, it is less clear whether they housed fugitives from slavery in their own homes. For example, Stephen Guthrie and his brother Austin were said to have been involved in helping William Harris, a Black man, hide a woman and four children in his home while the slave catchers were tricked into exploring an abandoned coal mine.

Unfortunately, the Harris house no longer exists. But a handful of other houses still stand that may well have served as stations on the Underground Railroad. For example, George Guthrie's Greek Revival house at 521 Woodlawn Avenue is believed to date to 1842–43. His wife, Sarah, wrote in her unpublished memoirs, "I well remember hiding three children in our attic over one Sabbath while their owners were riding through our streets in pursuit."[57]

Sarah was the daughter of Reverend Asa McFarland, who had performed the wedding of Daniel Webster and his first wife, as well as that of the painter and telephone inventor Samuel F.B. Morris. Sarah had

Major Horace and Lucinda Nye, prominent abolitionists in Muskingum County, lived in this house. *Courtesy Ford Walker.*

moved from New England to Putnam to become a teacher at Putnam Seminary. In 1973, local historian Norris F. Schneider noted that "the small door opening into the cavernous attic where the slaves were hidden still swings on the same hinges."[58]

Albert Austin Guthrie was known as "one of the most fearless Putnam conductors."[59] The corresponding secretary of the 1835 Ohio Anti-Slavery Convention, A.A. lived with his wife, Amelia, the sister of Solomon Sturges, at 405 Woodlawn Avenue. After the Stone Academy was overrun by a mob of Southern sympathizers, the planning meetings for the convention were moved to their home, which was built in 1820. Oral tradition has it that "when Guthrie's three daughters were told to go down the back stairs in the morning, they knew that the front hall upstairs contained runaway slaves."[60]

Another Sturges sister, Sarah, married Ebenezer Buckingham in 1812. She was his second wife. Ebenezer then invited her brother, Solomon Sturges, to move to Putnam and become his business partner. The brick Buckingham-Achauer house at 436–438 Putnam seems to have been built before the 1830s, possibly in 1820. Per Deed Book B in the county recorder's office, the lot on which the Buckingham-Achauer house was built was given to Ebenezer Buckingham by Rufus Putnam because Buckingham had married his daughter, Catherine, in 1805.

Amelia and A.A. Sturges, who lived in this home, were among the most brazen conductors in the local UGRR. *Courtesy Ford Walker.*

As Sarah's daughter, Kate (Sturges) Benton, later recalled:

> *I remember that when I was a little girl she* [Sarah] *hid in the dark depths of our big cellar several Negro families, fugitive slaves from Kentucky. She secreted and clothed, and fed them by day, and helped them forward by night on their journey to the Canadian border. How my heart thrilled with excitement, and how proud I was of my mother's courage.*[61]

The Buckinghams had also been brought up in the anti-slavery movement. Major Horace Nye, along with his wife, Lucinda (Belknap) Nye, were deeply involved in the abolitionist cause. He had presided over the 1839 state convention, while she was president of the Muskingum County Anti-Slavery Society. They were also alleged to have operated an Underground Railroad station out of their home at 228 Adams Street. "He kept his pitchfork within reach for weeks to defend himself against attacks from the Zanesville pro-slavery men."[62] Whether he ever harbored any fugitives there is unknown because he left no record of his activities.

Five people met in Springfield in 1807 to form a Congregational church. Two years later, they joined with some like-minded residents from across the river in Zanesville to form the Presbyterian Church of Zanesville and

Fugitives from slavery were purportedly hidden in the cellar of the Buckingham-Achauer House. *Courtesy Ford Walker.*

Springfield. After the Zanesville congregants grew tired of crossing the river to attend services, they split off, leaving the Putnam contingent to fend for themselves. The result was the Putnam Presbyterian Church, dedicated in 1835. From the beginning, the abolition of slavery was one of the congregation's core principles. How could it not be, with Reverend William H. Beecher, brother of abolitionist cleric Henry Ward Beecher and novelist Harriett Beecher Stowe, author of *Uncle Tom's Cabin*, as their minister?

The home of Nelson T. Gant and his wife, Anna Marie (Hughes) Gant, is located at 1845 West Main Street. At the time of his death in 1905, Gant was believed to be the wealthiest African American in Ohio. Born a slave on a tobacco plantation in Loudoun County, Virginia, in 1821, he was given his freedom on his master's death in 1845. He then had to raise money to purchase his wife from another slave owner in Leesburg. When he succeeded two years later, Nelson and Anna moved to Zanesville, where he set about building his fortune through hard work and shrewd business decisions.

Although Gant was said to have become a conductor on the Underground Railroad after meeting Frederick Douglass, there is little to go on other than tales that he concealed his runaways in his vegetable wagon in order to transport them from one station to another. And no evidence has surfaced that would indicate he hid any of the fugitives in his home. Of course, as a Black man, he would have had to be extra cautious to allay any suspicion. It would have made more sense for him to hide them elsewhere, since slave hunters were bound to come knocking on/kicking in his door. Obviously, it takes—or, rather, took—a village to conduct a UGRR operation, and Putnam is a good example.

"On Sunday, April 7, 1839, five mounted 'volunteer agents of Kentucky kidnappers' from nearby Georgetown rode to Brush Creek seeking Thomas Fox."[63] When Fox cried out for help, a handful of neighbors, including one White man, rushed to his aid. They demanded to see an arrest warrant, but the volunteers could not produce one and were forced to leave without him. Upper Camp, as the impoverished Brush Creek settlement was called, was the first of two in Brown County populated by the former slaves of Samuel Gist.[64] The other settlement was called Lower Camp. Both were places where people of color were welcome, whether free or not.

The following Sunday, April 14, some of the same men returned. This time they were accompanied by Constable Valentine Carberry and additional volunteers with an arrest warrant for Fox's neighbors, charging them with assault and battery. "The reinforced volunteers entered the settlement's church, dragged Moses Cumberland from his pew, and fought their way

George and Sarah Guthrie, whose home is pictured, were a driving force in the local abolitionist community. *Courtesy Ford Walker.*

to their horses through a group of angry parishioners, among whom Sally Hudson was most aggressive," according to the *Democrat and Herald*.[65]

One member of the church immediately set off for Sardinia to raise the alarm. Fifteen men from that anti-slavery community, led by Reverend John B. Mahan, jumped on their horses and raced to Brush Creek. Just a year before, Mahan had been kidnapped in Ohio and hauled down to Kentucky to stand trial on charges of helping slaves to escape.

About two miles from Brush Creek, the abolitionists encountered the would-be slave catchers. Constable Carberry later claimed Mahan's men threatened to shoot them if they did not turn Cumberland loose. When they refused, "a struggle ensued—the constable became alarmed, put spurs to his horse, and left the black man with his abolitionist friends."[66]

According to a letter to the editor of the *Ohio Statesman*, the impetus for arresting Fox was that he "had assaulted an individual."[67] However, this was thought to be a ruse to cover up slave catchers' real intent of carrying him back to slavery in Kentucky. The letter's author was clearly on the side of the slavers. When Fox was subsequently taken from the constable by "a band of desperadoes, headed by the notorious John B. Mahan, armed with pistols and club," the writer declared, "Thus you see the effects of the accursed doctrine of abolitionism."[68]

A day later, Carberry had Reverend Mahan and five of his companions placed under arrest on charges of riot and assault. Three were released by a Georgetown magistrate for lack of evidence, while Mahan and the other two were allowed to post bond. Then, on Sunday, April 21, another group of volunteers from Georgetown, joined by others from New Hope, made yet another visit to Brush Creek. This time, they were unable to find Fox or any of those who had frustrated their earlier attempt to capture him. So they changed their strategy.

As reported in the *Lebanon Star*, eighteen armed White men marched on the settlement at Brush Creek on Tuesday, April 30, 1839. They were confronted by "a number of colored persons, and two or three whites," determined to stop them from carrying out their plan.[69] In the ensuing skirmish, Sally Hudson, a Black woman, was singled out for punishment. Sally was the wife of John D. Hudson, a former slave who had been assisting runaway slaves since the 1820s. She "had allegedly struck at Grant Lindsey several times during his effort to take Moses Cumberland from the church on April 14. At one point she hit him hard of the nose."[70]

The volunteers beat Sally severely. When she tried to flee, "one of the men, James Kratzer, shot her in the back, shattering one of her vertebrae."[71] As Sally lay on the ground, mortally wounded, the fighting ended and the volunteers left, stunned by what had happened. The would-be abductors, "agents of Kentucky kidnappers, and citizens of Ohio," insisted they were acting in self-defense.[72] Although a Brown County grand jury refused to indict Hudson's killer, that September, a Georgetown jury convicted Reverend Mahan and the other Sardinians. They were sentenced to ten days in jail on bread and water.

In the spring of 1841, a Black man and his wife, Jefferson and Jane Johnson, were surprised by three slave hunters one Friday evening in a house in the forest a mile east of Oberlin, Lorain County. While the Johnsons likely were fugitive slaves, they had made a home for themselves in Oberlin, where Jefferson worked in a blacksmith's shop. Unwisely, he had shared too much of his story with a coworker, who passed the information along to a lawyer in Elyria named Judson Benedict. He then contacted the Johnsons' purported owner, notifying him where the runaways could be found.

When word of the kidnapping reached Oberlin College chapel, where a meeting was in progress, a party of men rushed to the couple's assistance. According to one southern newspaper, the mob consisted of five hundred people: "the students of the College and their associates, the negroes, armed with guns, clubs and stones."[73] Sherlock Bristol, an Oberlin student, was

Born into slavery, Nelson and Anna Gant built a fortune, as well as this home, through hard work and shrewd business decisions. *Courtesy Ford Walker.*

among those pursuing the slave catchers. "As tensions rose and guns were pointed, Bristol declared to his fellows: 'If they kill me, don't you leave one alive.'"[74] Fortunately, there was no violence, and the mob persuaded the Kentuckians to go to Elyria for a hearing.

Finding the slave hunters' paperwork to be "irregular," the magistrate, Judge Long, confined the Black man and woman in jail to allow their accusers time to return to Kentucky to obtain additional evidence in support of their claim. Immediately afterward, the Kentuckians were charged with assault and battery with deadly weapons and making threats to the occupants of the house in which the fugitives were found. As a result, Justice Birch bound two of them over to appear in court.

By some accounts, the slave owner was not with the slave hunters. By another, however, he was returning home to Kentucky to obtain more evidence when "he was suddenly grasped by the hand of death, and died within ten miles of Oberlin, with an oath upon his lips."[75] Furthermore, the Johnsons managed to escape. According to the *Cleveland Advertiser*, a mob of "students and other people of Oberlin" overran the jail, but those accused denied it.[76] Other sources say a basket maker who was also confined there managed to break out and they simply followed him. Consequently, the remaining slave hunter was released without trial.

The abolition of slavery was a core principle of the Putnam Presbyterian Church. *Courtesy Ford Walker.*

Many who escaped from slavery were strongly tempted to return to the South in hopes of rescuing their loved ones. Such celebrated UGRR heroes as Harriet Tubman and John Parker did so many times, risking their freedom and their lives. Others sometimes did so as well, with varying results.

A woman named Weeney Armstrong escaped from a Kentucky plantation in 1842 with her husband, Lewis, and a child. Eventually, the trio passed through Sandusky on their way to Canada. Two years later, however, the woman decided to return to Kentucky to retrieve seven other children she had left behind.

"Dressed as a man," Rush Sloane related, Mrs. Armstrong "reached her old plantation and hid at night near to a spring she knew her children visited early every morning."[77] As Weeney later told Levi Coffin, "[I] had not been there long before my eldest daughter came. I called her name in a low voice, and when she started up and looked round, I told her not to be afraid, that I was her mother."[78] They then hatched a plan for all the children to meet her at the spring the following evening at bedtime.

At the appointed hour, only five of the seven children showed up. The other two were sleeping in the master's room so that they could not slip away without being noticed. Nevertheless, Weeney set off with her children toward the Ohio River, some ten miles distant. Walking rapidly, they reached the river by early morning and crossed over to the Ohio shore on a skiff that was waiting for them.

"Going from station to station on the underground, [they] at length reached Sandusky, and after a short delay were safely forwarded and soon joined the husband and father and child…in Malden [Canada]."[79] Amazingly, Sloane was later informed "on good authority" that Mrs. Armstrong had returned to Kentucky once more and successfully retrieved her two remaining children.

Chapter 4

QUESTIONABLE QUILTS

Many women today enjoy making quilts. It's their medium of self-expression, their art form. But 175 years ago, it would have been the rare enslaved woman who felt that way. A typical reference to quilt-making in that era is this one taken from an interview with Fannie Moore, conducted in Asheville, North Carolina, in 1937:

> *My mammy she work in de fiel' all day and piece and quilt all night. Den she hab to spin enough three to make four cuts for de white fo'ks ebber night. Why sometime I nebber go to bed. Hab to hold de light for her to see by. She hab to piece quilts for de white folks too.…I never see how my mammy stan' sech ha'd work.*[30]

Obviously, this poor woman had little time to engage in any sort of recreational quilt-making for herself.

In 1989, Gladys-Marie Fry, professor emerita of folklore and English at the University of Maryland, published *Stitched from the Soul: Slave Quilts from the Antebellum South*. An African American, Fry was an authority on needlework produced by enslaved women and men. While the book's focus is on the many beautiful quilts, coverlets, rag rugs and crocheted artifacts she was able to locate, it is also a tribute to her great-great-grandmother Amanda, a quilt maker. Unfortunately, Fry was unable to locate any written records and only fragments of oral history regarding Amanda and her quilts.

Fry came to believe that quilts may have been used to identify safe houses and communicate other information to those who were making their way along the Underground Railroad. Ten years later, *Hidden in Plain View: The Secret Story of Quilts and the Underground Railroad* was published. Although the authors were White, their source wasn't. Their entire thesis was based on the oral testimony of African American quilt maker Ozella McDaniel Williams, who claimed that slaves crafted "coded" quilts that were then used to aid them when they escaped on the UGRR.

The tale Williams told went far beyond Fry's hypothesis. As a result, historian Giles R. Wright felt compelled to refute the premise of *Hidden in Plain View*. "Some black quilters have accused me of denying our heritage," Wright said. "I'm trying to protect it."[81] He noted that Williams's is a story that appears nowhere else in the hundreds—make that thousands—of slave narratives published or collected by innumerable researchers. His assumption is that Williams was putting the authors on in the interest of selling her quilts.

Wright picked apart the obvious flaws in such a "coded quilts" system. Although quilting parties were a common occurrence on the plantations, how was the ten-point quilt code (in which certain designs communicated specific instructions) created and by whom? How was it learned? How was using this code more effective than simply communicating information orally through the "grape-vine telegraph," as Booker T. Washington called it? Not to mention the fact that most quilters were elderly Black women who could no longer work in the fields, so where did they obtain their knowledge of the code? And for the most part, the quilts were made out of old clothing. It's not like the quilters had an abundance of time and materials to devote to quilt making.

The sheer inefficiency of such a system works against it, especially given that the focus of *Hidden in Plain View* is on Charleston, South Carolina, which "was not a major source of UGRR participants."[82] And those who did flee from South Carolina, Wright pointed out, were unlikely to head for Cleveland, Ohio, as the book suggests. Nevertheless, the story of Underground Railroad quilts has taken on a life of its own. Museums, libraries, churches and quilting groups continue to promulgate it, and regardless of whether it's true, teachers have incorporated the tale into their lesson plans.

Roland Freeman, a photographer and civil rights activist, asserted, "*Hidden in Plain View* is how we got over those white folks. Right under the nose of white folk we're sending signs and symbols and they don't know it. While I think it's so ridiculous, African Americans are starved for those kind

The Old Slave Market in Charleston, South Carolina, stands as a monument to human misery. *Courtesy of Brian Stanberry/Wikipedia.*

of stories in our culture and we're willing to accept it because it's what we want to hear."[83]

While few historians give the quilt code story any credence, especially since some of the "coded" quilt patterns didn't even appear until after the Civil War, there is always the possibility that it contains a kernel of truth. Perhaps someone, somewhere, did hang out a quilt to signify a safe house or as a navigational aid. But generally speaking, the only time quilts are mentioned in accounts of fugitive slaves was to keep them warm or conceal them from view. It is more likely that quilt makers used their art to commemorate the UGRR after the fact—showing where they had come from rather than where they were going.

The ghostwritten autobiography of Lewis and Milton Clarke provides an unusually detailed account of their many adventures as fugitives from slavery. They clearly relied on determination, happenstance and their own cunning in their flight to freedom rather than somebody else's directions.

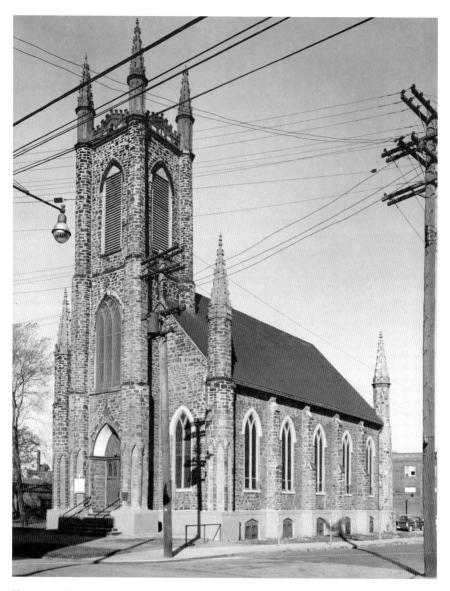

Known as Station Hope, St. John's Episcopal Church is Cleveland's first "authenticated" UGRR site. *Courtesy of Library of Congress.*

This was because, above all else, fugitives from slavery had to be flexible and opportunistic.

Milton had made his way from Kentucky to Oberlin, Ohio, and decided to stay there. However, it was not to be his permanent residence. As he related,

> *During the summer of 1841, the emigration to Canada, through Oberlin, was very large. I had the pleasure of giving the "right hand of fellowship" to a goodly number of my former acquaintances and fellow-sufferers. The masters accused me of stealing several of them. This is a great lie. I never stole one in my life. I have assisted several to get into possession of the true owner, but I never assisted any man to steal another away from himself.*[34]

That fall, Milton was delighted when Lewis joined him in Oberlin, having recently fled from his owner, a farmer named McGowan (or M'Gowan), in Kentucky. However, Lewis's master wasn't about to let him go so easily and began running newspaper ads offering a reward for his capture. One day, a young lawyer from Elyria named Chapman saw one of the ads. Knowing that the fugitive was living in Oberlin, he contacted McGowan and offered his assistance in apprehending him. In response, the slaveholder dispatched his son and a professional slave catcher named Postlewaite. When the two men arrived in Lorain County, they learned that the Clarke brothers had gone to the town of Madison in Lake County to visit Dr. Merriman and his family for a few days. So they went there as well, accompanied by Chapman.

Along the way, they encountered Milton riding with some members of the doctor's family. Catching him by surprise, they had no difficulty placing him under arrest and taking him before D.R. Paige, the associate justice of the county. Paige convened his court in a local tavern in Madison owned by J. Bliss. Lake County Sheriff Luther Bates was present and demanded to know what crime Milton was accused of. Postlewaite told him it was none of his business. The sheriff responded that it was and began to untie Milton. In response, "Postlewaite drew his pistols, and threatened to shoot him," while the judge warned the sheriff not to touch his property.[85]

As this scene was transpiring, the alarm had gone out that there were slave hunters about. The trial had yet to conclude when wagonloads of men began rolling into town, vowing that "no slave should be taken from Lake County."[86] What's more, a warrant had been sworn out before Judge Cunningham charging Postlewaite and McGowan with committing assault and battery on Milton Clarke.

No sooner had Judge Page ruled in favor of the slave catchers than Judge Cunningham's writ was served by Deputy Sheriff Jabeza A. Tracy. Tracy immediately conveyed Postlewaite and McGowan to the home of Cunningham, who lived on the Lake and Ashtabula County line. A procession of wagons, buggies and pedestrians followed them on both sides, in a highly agitated state of mind, toward Unionville. When they arrived in the village, there was a large crowd of people collected on the Lake County side of the road with their carriages, which prevented them from passing by without straying into Ashtabula County. Not wanting to cross the county line, which passed down the middle of the road, they tried to ride through the crowd. This prompted a fight.

Robert Harper, a Democrat who was trying to aid the slave hunters, stood on a dry goods box, read the riot act to the mob and tried to calm them down. However, he was in Lake County, so those in Ashtabula County weren't moved.

The Kentuckians drew their pistols and threatened to fire, but the mob stood its ground, "armed with fence-rails and other weapons hastily procured."[87] Judge Cunningham also begged them to put their guns away or the slave catchers would never make it back to Kentucky.

Among the spectators was a blacksmith who, according to Lewis, had taken the side of the slave hunters. But when some of Lewis's friends told him to identify the Black man, if there was one, he pointed at Postlewaite rather than Lewis and said, "That is the nigger."[88] Angered by the accusation, Postlewaite replied that "no man called him nigger with impunity."[89] An argument quickly ensued. After Postlewaite called him a liar three times, the blacksmith slapped him across the face. Postlewaite drew his bowie knife, threatening to cut the big man. So the blacksmith tore a sharp rail from a nearby fence and said he would cut him.

After half an hour of pushing and shoving and a plea by General Paine not to resort to violence, the party was forced to cross over into Ashtabula County. As soon as they did so, they were arrested by Sheriff John A. Prentiss on a writ of habeas corpus issued just that morning by a third judge, Jonathan Warner of Jefferson. Everyone then proceeded to Judge Cunningham's house. By then it was nearly dark, so the court was adjourned till the next day, "the prisoners giving bonds to be on hand at that time."[90]

For reasons of his own, Sheriff Prentiss kept Milton Clarke in custody rather than the slave catchers he had been instructed to arrest. Then, at nine o'clock that evening, he took Clarke from his cell and headed to Jefferson with the writ. A group of ardent abolitionists—Augustus Pepoon,

The route from Charleston to Cleveland was purportedly encoded on quilts to guide the freedom seekers. *Courtesy of Library of Congress.*

L.L. Rice, Philander Winchester and Seth Marshall—set out after them, ostensibly to ensure that they arrived safely. At the same time, George Fisher, a prominent Democrat from Madison, was dispatched to see that Milton did not escape.

Fisher "rode on horseback by the side of the teams almost to Jefferson, when, it being rather a dark night, he took the wrong road and became separated from the rest."[91] Sheriff Prentiss, after dropping Milton off at a tavern, rode off in search of the judge, leaving Milton with the abolitionists. "The assistant volunteers thought Milton might be lonesome," the author of a local history wrote, tongue firmly planted in cheek, "and asked him to take a ride with them."[92] Placing Milton in the wagon, they drove him to

Austinburg by a circuitous route and turned him over to Strong Austin, a committed abolitionist. No more was heard of Clarke until he turned up in Canada.

Clarke's rescuers packed the court the following morning, but Judge Cunningham had no choice but to acquit Postlewaite and McGowan of the assault charges when the key prosecution witness, Milton Clarke, failed to show up.

Nine fugitives from slavery arrived in Oberlin in 1842. All were purportedly from the Kentucky plantation of a man named Benningale, who was hot on their trail. The slave owner appeared in Oberlin the day after the runaway slaves and immediately stationed watchmen along the Lake Erie shore. Not only did Benningale offer a reward for anyone who provided him information, but he also threatened to burn down the village if he discovered the fugitives were hiding there.

The African American residents of Oberlin were particularly on guard. When they encountered a couple of men that evening whom they suspected of being spies for Benningale, they warned them that if they caught them out again, they would lynch them. As for the fugitives, they "were at length put into a wagon, carried to the lake, and shipped for Canada."[93]

Soon, seven more slaves, six men and a woman, made their way to Oberlin. According to the Clarkes' autobiography, "The miserable [lawyer] Benedict of Illyria [that is, Elyria], assisted by the Chapmans, set their traps around the village."[94] Having been sent a power of attorney by the fugitives' owner, Benedict offered a $700 reward for their arrest. However, the local abolitionists ensured that the slaves were kept well hidden. In order to move them to safety, they developed a plan to throw the slave hunters off their trail. Six Black men, including one named George, were chosen to impersonate the six male slaves, and Milton Clarke agreed to dress in women's clothing so he could impersonate the female slave.

A man the abolitionists knew would be certain to pass the information along to Benedict and the Chapmans was sworn to secrecy and told that "the slaves would start for the lake at such a time, and go in a certain direction."[95] He immediately hurried off to tell Benedict what he had heard. The seven decoys left Oberlin going in one direction, while the seven fugitives headed in another. As expected, Benedict, the Chapmans and the local sheriff went chasing after the decoys, bearing the writ "and all the implements of kidnapping."[96]

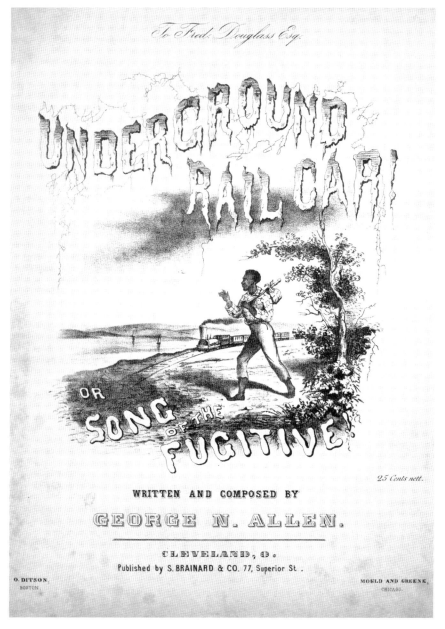

"Underground Rail Car," published in 1854 in Cleveland, was dedicated to "Fred Douglass, Esq." *Courtesy the Lester S. Levy Sheet Music Collection.*

Just as the decoys were arriving at Elyria, nine miles from Oberlin, their carriage was overtaken by the slave catchers, who ordered Platt, the driver, to stop. When Platt challenged Benedict's authority, the lawyer pulled out a copy of his advertisement, which described six men and one woman. Platt replied that he did not think his passengers were the persons Benedict was seeking. Benedict said he was certain they were. So turning to his passengers, Platt told them there was no more he could do for them.

According to Clarke, "George then began to play his part: 'Well, 'den, 'dis nigger must get out.'"[97] Following his lead, they all stepped down from the carriage and were escorted into a nearby tavern. Once inside, they were immediately asked where they were from. George responded that he didn't care where he was from.

By then, Benedict had begun to suspect that there was something amiss and decided to examine the female slave more closely. All the while, Clarke had kept his head and face hidden beneath the hood of his cloak. When Benedict ordered him to hold his head up, George told him, "Let 'dat gal alone, Mr. white man; de nigger gal plague enough in slave state—you just let her alone, here, if you please."[98]

By Clarke's account, George continued to talk and behave in a very impudent manner. When one of the slave hunters ordered a cider, George grabbed it and drank it down. When food arrived for them, George announced that he was hungry and "swept the table for himself and comrades."[99] And when the tavern keeper threatened to flog him, the other pretend slaves warned the man that he would do so at his own risk.

Finally, a justice of the peace arrived to conduct the hearing on the alleged runaway slaves. However, he had been let in on the secret. After Benedict presented his case and produced his evidence, noting that the female slave had left her mistress right in the middle of ironing her clothes, the justice ruled that he had no choice but to return the slaves to Benedict as fugitives from service.

"Our friends then gave the signal," Clarke related, "and I threw off my bonnet and cloak, and stood up a man. Such a shout as the spectators raised would do the heart of freedom good. 'Why, your woman has turned into a man, Mr. Benedict.'"[100] Then someone suggested that the others who appeared to be men might all be women. Realizing he had been played for a fool, Benedict immediately departed. The slave impersonators also left, returning to Oberlin in the carriage. "Meanwhile," Clarke concluded his story, "the real objects of pursuit were sailing on the waters of the blue lake."[101]

Chapter 5

THOU MAY BE MISTAKEN

S pring Hill was the home of Thomas (1767–1823) and Charity (Rodman) Rotch (1766–1824), a Quaker couple from New England who had moved to Ohio out of concern for Charity's fading health. Doctors had advised them to move south, but Ohio was as far south as they were willing to go given their strong objections to slavery. The Rotches had purchased an enormous parcel of land—2,600 acres—in the Ohio wilderness sight unseen with the intention of selling smaller tracts to other settlers. In doing so, they founded the village of Kendal, which later evolved into the city of Massillon.

There is no doubt that the Rotches were involved in local Underground Railroad activities. There is not only strong oral history but also documentation, some of which only came to light a century later. In William Perrin's 1881 *History of Stark County, Ohio*, the story is told of one such incident. In the spring of 1820, three fugitive slaves (a woman with two children) turned up at their door. Thomas put them up for the night in the second story of a nearby springhouse. Just after breakfast the next morning, a couple of strangers rode up and inquired if Mr. Rotch lived there. Told that he did, they revealed that they were hunting fugitive slaves.

After explaining that they had tracked the runaways to Rotch's home, the strangers showed Thomas a warrant for their arrest. Since Quakers were law-abiding people, De Camp, the leader, and his companion expected Thomas would hand over the mother and her children, albeit reluctantly.

Slave hunters were active in the vicinity of Massillon. *Courtesy of Wikipedia.*

"Dost thou think thou can take the woman and her children here if thou canst find them?" Thomas asked.[102]

De Camp replied that he did.

"Well," said Thomas, "thou may be mistaken. Thou hast not found them yet, and shouldst thou find them, thou might have trouble to take them."[103] As Thomas and the slave catchers were talking, three or four of Thomas's imposing farmhands had gathered around them.

"Dost thou know a man who follows the business of slave-catching by the name of De Camp?" Thomas asked.

"I do," De Camp replied. "Have you any business with me? My name is De Camp."

"I expect very soon to have some very important business with thee, and it will be well for thee to be prepared for it," Thomas answered.[104] With that, De Camp and his fellow slave catcher decided it would be prudent for them to depart.

It wasn't until more than a century later that an old pickle barrel stored in the wool house was discovered to contain a cache of documents dating back to the Rotch family. One of them was a three-page letter from George Duncan, Bainbridge, Geauga County, Ohio, to Thomas Rotch, dated August 14, 1820.

Duncan was a fugitive from slavery, believed to have been owned by Samuel Spriggs, an attorney and slave catcher from Wheeling, (West)

Virginia. He was writing to thank Thomas for his "trouble" and inform him that after leaving Kendal on his flight to Canada, he arrived safely in Geauga County and was being well treated by other opponents of slavery. He then asked Thomas to assist his wife, Edy, by not letting Spriggs know the road she would be taking. Furthermore, he suggested an alternative route to Bainbridge through Portage County that would likely avoid Spriggs. Duncan noted he was among "the yankee people and they are avowed enemies of Slavery."[105]

According to historian Dr. Roy E. Finkerbine, Duncan's mention of West Liberty refers to a community north of Wheeling. This was on a UGRR route followed by runaway slaves when they were crossing the Ohio River to Mount Pleasant, then to St. Clairsville and on to Massillon before continuing north to Lake Erie. Duncan also mentioned several other men, such as Martin and Elihu Kent, Quaker farmers who were apparently involved in the Ohio Underground Railroad, and John Bradays (likely Brady), with whom Edy was thought to be staying.

The significance of this letter is that it confirms the Rotches were involved in the Underground Railroad and that, in all likelihood, they welcomed Duncan into their home for a day. It also suggests that they assisted others,

Kendal's Spring Hill in Massillon is one of the best-preserved UGRR houses in Ohio. *Authors' collection.*

since Duncan did not hesitate to ask them to help his wife. In 1906, one W.R.E. of Short Hills, New Jersey, sent a letter to the *New York Times* in which he said he had a letter written by Charity (Rodman) Rotch to her sister, Anna (Rodman) Hazard, dated October 14, 1821. In the letter, Charity wrote,

The night before last we had a consignment of two negro men and a little boy fleeing for their liberty to Canada; poor things, they excited much sympathy and so prey upon my feelings that I should be glad to have but little of their company. We procured a man to go with them last night to put them on their way, the day having been mostly spent in providing food for them. About half an hour after they went a person knock'd at the door & who should it be but another negro of the same description; he was anxious, tho' very much fatigued, to overtake the others, & after provisioning another decoy we posted them away & were truly glad to be released so soon. This last man said he had been sold & was put on board a boat to go to New Orleans with a little boy 10 years old; the water was low in the river & at night he got off the boat undiscovered & traveled north. We were informed, by one of the persons that went, that he overtook the first party & they were travelling on, negro-like, apparently happy. He provided provisions to last them to Paynesville if they are only prudent. A very lamentable trait in the characters of a free people is the circumstances of the poor negroes in this land but I fear they will not be much better off in Canada.[106]

Spring Hill has several curious architectural features that may have been constructed specifically for UGRR activities, since the home was built after the Rotches had already started aiding fugitives from slavery. Originally, they concealed them in the upper story of their springhouse. But the new house had two stairways leading up from the cellar. One is a conventional stairway; the other is a steep, twisting one that does not stop until it reaches the second floor. From there, it opens into a hallway with a closet that held a barrel of sugar concealing a doorway that leads to a crawlspace above the first floor. Whether the Rotches used these stairways to hide runaways, however, is unknown, and the Spring Hill Association is careful not to mislead the public. Even without the Underground Railroad connection, it would be an important historic site.

An hour or two after midnight on October 30, *1842*, a band of well-armed slave hunters, perhaps as many as a dozen, forced their way into the home of Vincent Wigglesworth on Big Indian Road, Moscow, Ohio. After tying him up, they carried his wife and his four children back to Kentucky.

On the second floor of Spring Hill, a small attic door was hidden behind a large sugar barrel. *Authors' collection.*

Another small door on the second floor led to a beehive in the attic. *Authors' collection.*

For the past sixteen years, Vincent, a freedman, and his wife, Fanny (her legal status is unclear), had resided in a house about four miles from the Ohio River. Their children (Maryann, age fifteen; Eliza, ten; Josiah, five; and a female infant age sixteen days) were all freeborn. In all that time, the Wigglesworths had never experienced any trouble.

The following Friday, some citizens of Clermont County convened a meeting at Calvary Methodist Church. A newspaper reported that they adopted resolutions empowering the committee "to take such steps for apprehension of the kidnappers, and for the recovery of the family stolen, as they shall deem proper."[107] Their outrage, however, was tempered by their respect for the law—the law that protected the rights of slave owners.

"When slaves so escaping are sought to be reclaimed in a lawful manner," the ad hoc committee noted, "we have never interfered."[108] The committee also asserted that "the complaint sometimes made by the citizens of Kentucky, of our unwillingness to surrender up fugitive slaves when demanded by their owners, is utterly unfounded."[109] That was the group's public stance, but Clermont County was known to be an abolitionist stronghold.

Robert E. Fee, operator of a Moscow hotel, was subsequently hired by Ohio Governor Thomas Corwin and his brother, Robert, to track down Fanny and her children and bring them home. But the kidnappers, William Moore and William Middleton, had "dispersed the five family members, [so] Fee was unable to locate them during his search of Ohio and Missouri."[110]

Although Wigglesworth engaged a well-known Ohio attorney to secure an indictment and extradition orders against Moore and Middleton, they were never brought to justice. Neither were Fanny and her children ever recovered. It was likely they had been sold into slavery in Platte County, Missouri.

As for Robert Fee, he was beaten by a proslavery mob while searching for the Wigglesworths. Afterward, "he and his family, including his daughters, slept with loaded firearms in ready reach, and…Fee burned a light in his window at night to assist any runaways."[111] Ten years later, Fee was purportedly indicted on a charge of slave stealing by a grand jury in Pendleton County, Kentucky, but Governor Reuben Wood of Ohio, a Democrat, refused to extradite him.

As far as is known, the Reverend William M. Mitchell was the only person to write a book about the Underground Railroad while the UGRR was illegal. Published in 1860, *The Under-Ground Railroad* provides an account of the author's activities on a "Vigilance Committee" aiding fugitives from slavery in their escape to Canada. Mitchell related that he "was initiated into the underground business in the county of Ross, in the State of Ohio, in 1843, and continued in the office, faithfully discharging the duties, until 1855."[112]

Mitchell wrote that his introduction to the Underground Railroad occurred in 1843, sometime after his arrival in Ohio, presumably in southern Ross County. He learned that a fugitive slave who had escaped from Maryland had settled in the area, protected by the local Methodist church. However, several years later, the minister of the church decided to betray the fugitive's whereabouts in order to collect the hundred-dollar reward that had been offered by his owner for his recapture. While the runaway, a married father of three, was at work, "three men came suddenly upon him, put a rope around his neck, and unceremoniously dragged him beyond the limits of the Town Authorities, and on to his former place of Slavery."[113]

But not quite. About two hundred members of the "Coloured Community" rallied to his aid and overtook the slave catchers about three miles outside of town. The men were on horseback, and the fugitive was tethered to the neck of one of the horses. "When it became apparent to them that their own liberty and security were in danger, they cut the rope from the neck of the steed, and spurring their horses, they were soon out of our reach and sight."[114] However, their quarry had been saved.

While traveling to Wheeling, (West) Virginia, in 1843, D.P. Scanlan of New Orleans stopped off in Cincinnati for a visit. He was accompanied by his wife and daughter, as well as a nine- or ten-year-old slave girl named Lavinia, who served as his daughter's nurse. Before Lavinia left on the trip, her mother told her she would punish her if she did not try to escape once she reached Ohio. She also promised to join her if she could and placed a small gold chain around her neck so she would recognize her daughter.

Once in Cincinnati, Lavinia looked for an opportunity to separate herself from the Scanlans. On Wednesday, August 2, 1843, she met an African American couple who took her home until evening. They then placed her in the safekeeping of Samuel Reynolds, a Quaker, who lived in a house near the foot of Sycamore Hill. The following evening, Lavinia was taken in by a lady whose husband was "absent from home at the time, and knew nothing of the matter until the child had been for some time under his roof," according to the *Cincinnati Enquirer*.[115] Although Scanlan went to the house in search of the girl, he was unaware that Lavinia was hiding under a trundle bed. Returning later with some friends, he was met by Reynolds, who bought some time by suggesting that they meet at the house of one H. Lewis to discuss the matter.

Even though he agreed, Scanlan did not attend the meeting. Instead, he assembled his friends with the intent of searching the house by force. But Lavinia was relocated to the nearby home of abolitionists Edward Harwood and John H. Coleman. Nevertheless, Scanlan found the fugitive and would have made off with her if it weren't for the growls of Swamp, a large watchdog. The following night, Scanlan returned, boldly entered the house and demanded the surrender of the young girl.

When Scanlan was unable to find her, he retreated to the Alhambra Saloon, where he gathered a group of rowdy men to aid in Lavinia's recovery. However, Harwood and Coleman had also recruited some friends of their own. "Finally a large crowd gathered about Coleman's house headed by an officer notorious for his zeal in capturing slaves," according to a local historian.[116] Although the officer sought to enter the house, Coleman turned him away because he did not have a search warrant. As the mob grew, energized by liquor and inflammatory speeches, the abolitionists filled the house with guns and ammunition, preparing for the worst.

"The sheriff of the county, John H. Gerard, had been appealed to for protection by the Colemans," Cincinnati historian Charles Grieve later wrote, "but he had refused any assistance with the statement that if they made themselves obnoxious to their neighbors they must suffer the consequences."[117] As this was playing out, Harwood, Coleman and several other men smuggled Lavinia out of the house and down the hill to the home of a Mr. Emery.

Although the mob continued to rage and howl in the streets for hours, they dared not attack the house because they knew there were thirty or forty well-armed men waiting inside. Finally, they marched on the home of Cornelius Burnett, who was "represented to be a notorious Abolitionist and busy body."[118] They began hurling stones and brickbats at the dwelling, breaking the front windows. Before more serious damage could be done, however, Henry E. Spencer, the mayor of Cincinnati, arrived with the Watchmen—those who were authorized to stand watch on the city streets at night—and arrested several rowdies and ringleaders. Still, a mob remained throughout the night, throwing rotten eggs and other missiles at Burnett's house.

The following evening, Mayor Spencer, who had been struck in the side by a brickbat, ordered out the military to quell the mob. Lavinia remained at the Emery home for a week or so, masquerading as a young boy. Finally, she slipped out with some boys who were driving cows out to pasture and was escorted to a station on the UGRR. From there, she was conveyed to Oberlin, "where she received a good education, [and] proving to be a woman of good ability and much intelligence, she was sent as a missionary to Medina mission in Africa," Levi Coffin would recall.[119]

About 1845, a "General McCansland" (possibly McCausland) and a posse of slave catchers swept into Gallia County in pursuit of five fugitives from his plantation in Mason County, (West) Virginia. He trailed them to the home of Hiram Davis, a local farmer who was actively involved in the Underground Railroad. According to Professor Siebert, "Davis hid the slaves in a small hole under his house, with the only access to the chamber being through a small door in the floor of the home."[120] He covered the door with a carpet and then placed a large loom on top of it.[121]

As McCansland and his men approached, Davis watched from a window adjacent to the front door. When the general told him he was looking for his slaves, Davis, who stood more than six feet in height, warned him that if anyone tried to enter his house, he would slay them with an axe. Although the slave catchers surrounded the home so no one could leave, none of them dared venture inside. Meanwhile, three or four women who were in the house began boiling water, which they planned to toss on anyone who tried to gain entry.

It wasn't long before a crowd numbering nearly two hundred gathered to watch the standoff. One of them, a Mrs. Griffin, boldly entered the Davis home, carrying two guns and a generous supply of ammunition. "She instructed the women to add cornmeal to the boiling water, believing that it would stick better to and cause more harm to the intruders," Siebert related.[122]

Finally, a constable arrived, undoubtedly summoned by McCansland. Although he carried a search warrant, Davis refused to admit him, and he soon left. But Davis did agree to allow McCansland, a local judge and an attorney to conduct a search of the premises. Failing to detect the secret chamber, they were unable to find any of the fugitives, so they left empty-handed. The five freedom seekers then continued on their journey north.

Chapter 6

GOODBYE, JOCKO GRAVES

There is a surprisingly diverse group of people who are united behind the declaration that some cast-iron statues of Black men, particularly those known as Jockos, once served a noble purpose. Unfortunately, that was the belief of the late historian Charles L. Blockson, curator of the Afro-American Collection at Temple University in Philadelphia, despite a conspicuous lack of evidence. "These statues were used as markers on the Underground Railroad throughout the South into Canada," Blockson assured Pamela Sherrod of the *Chicago Tribune*.[123] Green ribbons were allegedly tied to the arms of the statues to signal when it was safe to stop and red ribbons when it wasn't.

However, Blockson's assertion does not stand up to scrutiny. To begin with, the use of red and green—originally red and white—to indicate *stop* or *go* did not emerge until late in the nineteenth century, in conjunction with railroad signals. And since most fugitive slaves traveled under cover of darkness, they would have found it difficult to even see the ribbons, let alone identify their colors.

Likely because he was a prominent African American, Blockson's opinion is frequently quoted by defenders of the grotesque and undeniably racist-looking Jocko figures. He also was the proud owner of one. In contrast to the white "Cavalier Spirit" statues, which were more idealized depictions of jockeys, the Jockos are hunched over and wide-eyed, with exaggerated lips and flat noses. Many are painted shiny black. It's like all African American stereotypes combined in one figure.

A "Jocko" as pictured on the cover of Professor Wilbur H. Siebert's book. *Authors' collection.*

Wilbur H. Siebert's *Mysteries of Ohio's Underground Railroad* includes an image of a vintage Jocko. It is tied to an article in the Springfield *News-Sun* that reported how Mrs. Benjamin M. Piatt of Logan County "utilized a little statue of a Negro to signal whether the slaves could be left safely."[124]

Elizabeth Piatt purportedly hid the runaways in their eighteen-room log home, which stood opposite Mac-a-Cheek Castle. Sensitive to her husband's position as a "federal judge," however, she only did so when he was away. To communicate it was safe to stop, she placed a tiny American flag in the hand of a statue, which had once been used to hold a rope when a steamboat was tied up on the Ohio River. But is it true?

Several sources state that Benjamin Piatt was a "Federal Circuit Judge" or a "U.S. District Court Judge." But Howe's *Historical Collections of Ohio* records that he was appointed to fill a vacancy on the common pleas bench in Hamilton County sometime after he arrived in Cincinnati. A *History of Cincinnati and Hamilton County* lists him as an associate judge of the court of common pleas from 1823 to 1826. Soon thereafter, he moved to Logan County, where he built his log home. There is no mention of any other judgeships.

Wilbur Siebert learned of an incident involving Judge Piatt and some runaway slaves that calls into question exactly where the Piatts stood on the issue of slavery. Judge William H. West of Bellefontaine related that in November 1852, a trio of slaves belonging to members of the Piatt family in Kentucky boarded a train somewhere between Cincinnati and West Liberty. They were soon recognized by Donn Piatt, son of Benjamin. Removing them from the train, Donn took them to his father's home, where they were held until their owner could claim them.

An elderly Black man named Arthur Ash took it upon himself to apply to Judge West for a writ of habeas corpus. West and his legal partner, Judge James Walker, took the case to probate court, where it was heard by Judge E. Bennett. According to West, "The old gentleman [that is, Benjamin] Piatt resisted the discharge of the negroes and talked against time, stating whose slaves they were, but the proceedings were hurried and the fugitives were discharged before the coming in of the train bearing the [U.S.] marshall

A vintage photo of the Benjamin Piatt cabin before it was restored. *Authors' collection.*

[*sic*]."[125] Through Judge Bennett's quick action, the three fugitives were able to evade the marshal and reach Canada.

So if Elizabeth Piatt were operating a UGRR safe house, it would seem to have been without Benjamin's knowledge and approval. After war broke out, however, Judge Piatt became a Republican and threw all his support behind preserving the Union.

Historian Kate Clifford Larson discovered that the "Jockos" (or lawn jockey statues, as they later came to be called) were first manufactured around 1864–65. They were originally "hitching posts in the form of an enslaved boy, in tattered clothes, sitting atop a bale of cotton with his hand outstretched with a ring to hitch a horse. They were sold primarily in the New Orleans market (then occupied by the Union [army]."[126] This was the style best known as the "faithful groomsman."

The figures evolved over the ensuing years. By the 1870s, they "had taken the form of a black groomsman. The statue was known variously as the 'Sambo Hitching Post,' 'Negro Boy Hitching Post,' and 'Nigger Hitching Post.'"[127] They did not come to be called "lawn jockeys" until the twentieth century. One such figure was manufactured by the New Bremen Foundry & Machine Company, New Bremen, Ohio, which existed from 1881 to 1890, just after the era of Reconstruction in the South.

Donn Piatt, son of Judge Benjamin Piatt, attempted to start an unauthorized brigade of all Black soldiers during the Civil War. *Library of Congress.*

Surprisingly, it was two African American businessmen who did the most to create the legend surrounding the lawn jockeys and give "Jocko" its name. In 1963, Earl Koger Sr. published the story of Jocko Graves, a twelve-year-old African American youth who wanted to join General George Washington in fighting the British forces the night Washington crossed the Delaware River. Because Jocko was too young for combat, Washington purportedly asked him to hold their horses and keep a lantern burning so they could find him again.

But on his return hours later, Washington discovered that Jocko had frozen to death, still gripping the lantern in his icy fist. So to honor the memory of Jocko, Washington commissioned a sculpture of his "faithful groomsman" and installed it at his Mount Vernon estate. Again, there is a dearth of evidence. No records exist of Jocko Graves, the purported statue or a person freezing to death while tending Washington's horses.

Nevertheless, Koger's story was subsequently adapted for a children's opera. Then a friend of Koger's, Waymon Lefall, further perpetuated the Jocko story in a couple more books, one for children. Both men were interested in promoting racial pride.

In 1982, syndicated newspaper columnist Ann Landers used her resources in an effort to uncover the truth about Jocko Graves. After checking with everyone from the managing editor of *Ebony* magazine to the Pennsylvania Historical Society, she arrived at Ellen McCallister, librarian at Mount Vernon. McCallister replied, "I am aware of the story, and it is pure fiction. George Washington kept a list of all his slaves, and Jocko Graves does not appear on the list. Washington also faithfully recorded the historical events that occurred in his lifetime, and this tale is not among them."[128] Of course, a few inconvenient facts seldom change anyone's mind, and there will be those who continue to proudly display their Jocko statues and insist that anyone who is offended by them is the true racist.

TWO SLAVES ESCAPED FROM Wood County, (West) Virginia, on Saturday night, February 6, 1847, and made their way to Ohio. One of them belonged to J. Tumbleson and the other to G. Henderson. The following day, they were believed by some to have found refuge in the home of David Putnam Jr. in Harmar, Washington County, about a mile away across the Ohio River. Putnam was the great-grandson of Major General Israel Putnam, a hero of the American Revolution who was known for leading from the front, not from behind. David Putnam Jr. was cast from the same mold.

A watch was placed on Putnam's house, and by late Sunday evening, a large crowd of men had encircled it, vowing not to allow the slaves to get away. "A great deal of disturbance was made," the *Marietta Intelligencer* reported, "and it is also alleged that threats of violence were uttered."[129] Not only were there a number of men assembled from Wood County, but a message had also been sent to Parkersburg seeking reinforcements. Soon the rumor spread throughout Harmar that a mob was threatening to destroy Putnam's home.

"As might have been expected, a multitude soon collected and dispersed watchers in double quick time," the *Intelligencer* reported. "Whether all who aided in keeping peace would have done so if they credited the report that the Negroes were really in Putnam's charge is questionable."[130] Yet the size of the mob apparently worked to the slaves' advantage, for during "the hubbub the Negroes were dressed up in cloaks, marched through the crowd, furnished with horses, and started post haste for Queen Victoria's dominions."[131]

Two years later, Putnam was sued by George Washington Henderson of Briar Plantation, Williamstown, [West] Virginia, in the U.S. District Court in Columbus "for the loss of nine slaves, which Henderson claimed Putnam had influenced to run away."[132] There were at least seventeen known

A "faithful groomsman" was given to Ohioan Louis Bromfield by fellow author Edna Ferber and stood in front of his Malabar Farm home for many years. *Authors' collection.*

instances of slaves escaping from Briar Plantation. Those involving Putnam allegedly occurred between February 15, 1846, and February 11, 1847. In the first of two suits, Henderson sought $5,500 in compensation for the loss of the nine slaves. In the second suit, he asked for $10,000 in compensation for Putnam causing a breach of contract and for lost labor and legal fees. Both suits were in litigation for three years before they were dismissed due to the changes that had come about as a result of the enactment of the new Fugitive Slave Law in 1850.

An enslaved man named Roberts and a woman he later married escaped from (West) Virginia near Point Pleasant in 1848 by concealing themselves in a boat that was passing up the Ohio River. They finally landed near Steubenville, on the Ohio side, and continued on foot until they reached the small town of Randolph, Portage County, on the southern edge of the Western Reserve. "Here they found some friends," one county history records, "and concluded to stop and go to work, in order to replenish their means to enable them to pursue their flight to Canada."[133]

The couple thought they would be safe, but about two weeks later, several strangers arrived in the village. They pretended to be interested in buying land and other such matters, but the residents of the small community were suspicious. It wasn't long before the two men climbed in their carriage and started off toward the place where the fugitives were working.

One young man jumped on his horse and caught up with the strangers. After engaging them in a brief conversation, he rode ahead to warn Roberts and the woman of the approaching danger. They took refuge in a nearby house, concealing themselves in an upper room. When the men arrived, the owner of the house met them at the gate and began to question them. But they would not reveal their mission. "Very soon the people of the surrounding country commenced dropping in to take a view of the strangers, whom they already began to mistrust belonged to a class of bipeds called manstealers."[134]

During the next hour, about one hundred farmers from vicinity had assembled. The two men finally stated their purpose and asked permission to speak with Roberts and his companion. "By this time the strangers began to discover some very decided manifestations of displeasure among the crowd, as some of them had been so indiscreet as to bring with them old rifles and muskets, from which an occasional pop would be heard in the distance."[135] As night approached, the slave hunters retired to a local hotel.

All night long, local citizens stood guard outside the hotel to ensure the men did not venture out. The next day, the strangers decided there was no point in remaining, so they called for their horses and prepared to return to (West) Virginia. As they left town, nearly two hundred people followed them just to ensure they didn't change their minds. That night, the friends of Roberts and his companion met to discuss the best course of action. Fearing that the slave hunters might return with reinforcements, they decided it would be best to convey them some fifty miles to the village of Concord. But before doing so, they saw to it that the couple was married. "These fugitives were never after molested, but remained in this neighborhood" of Concord until 1852, when they fled to Canada.[136]

AN ENSLAVED MAN NAMED Asa who worked as a blacksmith for Kentuckian John P. Campbell ran away in the summer of 1848. Campbell subsequently learned that Asa "had taken up his abode within six or seven miles of Ripley, on the Ohio River."[137] Accompanied by several other men, Campbell went to Ohio, where he found his bond servant working at his blacksmith shop. He was going by the name Bishop.

According to ex–Kentucky governor Thomas Metcalfe, when Campbell and the others attempted to arrest Asa, they were foiled by the intervention of some abolitionists, and the slave started running away. "He fled in the presence and with the plaudits of numerous admiring spectators, crying aloud, 'Run, Bishop! Run, Bishop! Run, Bishop!'"[138]

Two White men—"White outside," Metcalfe asserted—ran beside Asa, helping him to escape. One of them handed him a pistol, with which he shot one of Campbell's men. However, the one-ounce pistol ball was deflected by a pair of handcuffs in the man's pocket, so he was not injured. The slave hunters returned fire, and the fugitive was slightly wounded. When he was about to collapse from exhaustion, the men who were aiding his escape mounted him on a horse, and he rode away.

Campbell returned to Ohio a month or so afterward to resume his hunt but was frustrated by his inability to find a marshal or commissioner willing to help him. According to Metcalf, a commissioner in Cincinnati "expressed doubts as to his authority to deputize another to act out of his own county—the county of Hamilton—notwithstanding the information he had previously received from Judge [John] McLean, that he had the power to make such an appointment."[139]

The result was Campbell was delayed several hours searching for Judge McLean, and when he found him he had not further difficulty in effecting his object—his honor, like the rest of the patriotic class of which he is a distinguished member, having determined to fulfil every legal and constitutional obligation due to his country—his whole country.[140]

Meanwhile, Asa's trail had gone cold. Campbell resolved to sue everyone who had a hand in helping the slave escape. He believed Asa was "still secreted by the fanatics."[141] A Ripley newspaper even called Campbell's pursuit of Asa an "act of felony."[142] For his part, Metcalfe lamented the "depredations committed upon our rights by the people of Ohio, by the direst non-fulfillment of legal and constitutional obligations."[143] Known as Stonehammer because he used to be a stonemason, Metcalfe had helped build Kentucky's first governor's mansion when he was younger. Opposed to limitations of any kind on the expansion of slavery in the United States, he once said, "They may say what they like about my views, but the first man that dares to attack my character, I will cleave his skull with my stone hammer, as I would cleave a rock."[144]

Chapter 7

PAP'S DIARY

S alem, Ohio, was platted by Quakers from Salem, New Jersey, in 1806, and was abolitionist to its core. Although the *Anti-Slavery Bugle* was founded in nearby New Lisbon in 1845, the newspaper moved to Salem after the first five issues came off the press. The *Bugle*'s motto was No Union with Slaveholders. Published by James Barnaby, the paper survived for eighteen years, circulated throughout the United States, and put Salem on the map when it came to the campaign against slavery.

For a town with a population of fewer than nine hundred, Salem was punching above its weight. Then, in 1849, a splinter group of Quakers called the Progressive Friends came together in order to devote more of their resources toward abolishing slavery and promoting women's rights. Daniel Howell Hise and his wife, Margaret Goulbourn Hise, were at the forefront of these and similar issues, donating both their time and money.

On those occasions when he was offered the opportunity to be a leader, however, Hise declined if the position required that he swear an oath to uphold the Constitution of the United States. There were simply too many provisions of that governmental charter with which he disagreed. For instance, he believed that women and people of color should have the right to vote, and since they didn't, he abstained from voting as well.

When Professor Wilbur Siebert interviewed George W.S. Lucas, an African American, about his connection to the Underground Railroad, Lucas related that "Philip Evans and Howell Hise and Dr. Carey—all of Salem—knew me and were acquainted with the U.G.R.R. work. These

The John Street House on North Ellsworth in Salem was purportedly connected by a tunnel to another house across the street. *Authors' collection.*

men kept the fugitives, who generally came here from across the Ohio river, from Wellsville and Cadiz."[145] Lucas added that when he was transporting fugitives to Lake Erie, "Friends would write to Hise or Evans to warn him from what port to ship."[146]

Hise first wrote of his involvement with fugitives from slavery on April 8, 1849, nearly two years after he began keeping a diary. Pap's diaries (Pap was his nickname) are important source documents, covering over thirty-one years of Salem social history. There are several different transcriptions of them, which differ slightly due to the difficulty in deciphering Hise's handwriting, spelling and punctuation.

Judging by his entries, Hise's involvement in Underground Railroad activities was sporadic. The first recorded incident was on April 8, 1849, when seven fugitives arrived at seven thirty in the evening. "Welcome, welcome to the protection I can give with or without law," Hise wrote.[147] Presumably, he put them up at his house or shop. The next mention of the UGRR was on April 22, when he "met some fugitives and met with them for some time sitting in a publick [*sic*] place."[148] Four days later, he attended a secret Underground Railroad meeting and then went to Thomas Harner's to pick up a fugitive. He planned to take him to another neighborhood around midnight.

Quaker Calvin Moore's house on South Lincoln purportedly had a secret room where he hid freedom seekers. *Authors' collection.*

On February 5, 1850, there was "great excitement in town today in consequence of the arrival of some slave holders."[149] They spotted three of the runaways, so Hise "secreted" one, named George, "in the country until the excitement" was over. The "country" may have been a reference to the Cattell house on Jennings Avenue. Then, on December 15, "Four fugitive slaves arrived at ten o'clock, three of whom were from Virginia, the other from New Orleans."[150] The fourth "stopped" with Hise.

Ten months later, early on the morning of October 17, 1851, Hise transported eight slaves who were on the run from Parkersburg, (West) Virginia, to the home of D. Bonsalls. They had been brought to him by Charles Grizzell at midnight. One of them was well armed with a knife and a brace of pistols. Then, on March 23, 1852, Elwood Vickers borrowed Hise's carriage to drive a fugitive to another station. After that, there was a considerable lull in activity.

The most famous incident Hise participated in occurred on August 28, 1854. The Western Antislavery Society was concluding its annual convention in the Hicksite Quaker Church. "At about 3 o'clock in the afternoon a telegram was received in Salem stating that a train bearing a slaveholder, his wife and a girl slave, had left Pittsburgh for the west and would pass through the town at 6 o'clock that afternoon," according to historian Charles Galbreath.[151]

When the convention speaker received the message, he read it to the audience. He then challenged them to act on their principles by rescuing the slave. Some thirty of them set out to do so. As the news spread throughout the town, the convention delegates were joined by many local citizens. They reached the railroad depot ahead of the train and were further encouraged by several of their number, who improvised speeches. They then appointed a committee to board the train. The committee included a Black man from Salem in the belief that the slave girl would be more likely to trust him.

At six o'clock, the train arrived, and the committee quickly climbed aboard. Four of Hise's associates spotted an African American girl they thought to be about twelve and asked a man in her vicinity if she was really a slave. The man replied that she was and that she belonged to him. They then asked the girl, "Do you desire to be free?" and she replied, "Yes."[152] No sooner had she spoken than the abolitionists picked her up and carried her off.

Despite the slave owner and his wife's loud protests, the couple soon departed without her for Tennessee—but not before leaving behind her clothes. That evening, the girl was placed on the rostrum at the antislavery convention, led by a White girl her own age. "The meeting reached its appropriate climax when the little girl was again brought forward and

This Salem mansion on South Lincoln is said to have been another of a handful of safehouses. *Authors' collection.*

Liebe Winery on State Street in Salem was previously Jacob Heaton's home and dry goods store, where fugitives from slavery were purportedly concealed. *Authors' collection.*

named 'Abby Kelley Salem,' after the famous Quaker woman [Abby Kelley Foster] whose oratory had done so much to advance the anti-slavery cause in the West."[153] The conventioneers also collected fifty dollars to defray the cost of clothing her and providing her with an education. For a time, Abby lived with the family of Joel McMillan and was accorded many of the advantages enjoyed by White children.

On October 12, Hise and other abolitionists went to the depot early to greet a group of five fugitives from slavery. "They all got off," he wrote. "No one was with them to molest them or make them afraid."[154] A year later, on October 30, 1855, the citizens of Salem armed a fugitive slave so that he could defend himself. "I gave what I thought was my share," Hise noted. "I am for open hostility"—not exactly a Quaker attitude.[155] These were pretty much Hise's last words on his Underground Railroad work.

Hise took possession of the home he named Unserheim (German for "our home") on February 17, 1857, and moved out of Salem, where he had lived for the past thirty-eight years. Although extravagant claims have been made that he built this new house with fifty windows, seven doors and six stairways just to confuse slave hunters and also included secret rooms for hiding the fugitives, his diary does not support any of these.

Historian Cris Swetye pointed out that Hise "recorded [in his diary] the existence of only 17 fugitive slaves in the 13 years before the Civil War."[156] So either he deliberately omitted some stories or there weren't any others.

The following incident occurred near Belpre, Washington County. According to a Belpre historian:

> *In 1850 a company of six or seven negroes were piloted from Francis Stone's one night by Mr. Vickers just beyond the twin bridges. At that time Mr. Smith was building the abutment of the bridge at the mouth of Davis Creek. The next morning Mr. I.W. Putnam, noticing that Mr. Smith was late at breakfast remarked that he must have been running negroes away.*[157]

He was right. At the time, a large group of slaves—men, women and children—had fled from (West) Virginia. They made their way to the farm of Massa Hovey on Duck Creek, about fifteen miles from Marietta, with their pursuers following closely behind. Aided by sympathetic locals, they entered a deep ravine on Hovey's farm and hid themselves behind a fallen tree.

"There they were kept for three weeks," J.W. Tuttle recalled, "while the woods in the vicinity were searched for them by their owners and the 'lick spittle' hired to aid in the search"—*lickspittle* being a name given to those willing to help slave catchers in exchange for a reward.[158]

While the search was underway, two of the lickspittles were given money by the slave hunters to buy whiskey and tobacco. Taking their rifles, the two men decided to hunt not only runaways but also squirrels. One of them shot a squirrel that was in the top of a tree, and it fell down among the fugitives, who were in hiding behind the fallen tree. Fortunately, as the shooter was starting to retrieve it, his companion said, "Come on we are hunting niggers."[159] So they left without it, and the band of escapees was not discovered.

Over the course of three weeks, the fugitives were secretly furnished with food and water. Finally, Randal S. Wells from Middle Creek, Monroe County, led them to Canada, where they all arrived safely. In September the same year, Congress passed the Fugitive Slave Act of 1850, which made the federal government, as well as all citizens, responsible for the apprehension and return of escaped slaves. Even those who opposed slavery were now obligated to help slaveholders recover their "property."

Following emancipation from slavery, Alabama basket maker Strotter Brown plied his trade in Salem. *Authors' collection.*

FORMERLY ENSLAVED IN MISSOURI, Lewis Hutson was set free in his master's last will and testament. But the master's sons were determined not to surrender ownership of this valuable commodity and made every effort to break the will. Fearing they might succeed, Hutson set out for Ohio sometime between 1848 and 1851. The sons did not know where to look for him. However, one of them chanced to encounter the fugitive on the waterfront while visiting Cincinnati.

After exchanging pleasantries with the runaway, the son and his brothers hatched a plan to seize Hutson at night and smuggle him across the river to Kentucky. From there, they would take him to the Deep South, presumably to sell. As he was leaving for work one evening, Hutson was "pounced upon by a gang of kidnappers," operating under the direction of the son.[160] "Receiving no help from any quarter," Reverend William Troy related, "he was conveyed across the river to the slave State, Kentucky, and, chained and handcuffed, was put on board one of the Southern steamboats for the slave-market in New Orleans."[161]

Once underway, however, Hutson prevailed on the African American deckhands to provide him with a small boat so he could make his escape. One night, they did, and he was soon adrift on the Mississippi, unable to use the oars because of the handcuffs he wore. Fortunately, the wind drove his boat ashore, where he waded through a "reed-marsh." Despite the presence of crocodiles and other animals, Hutson remained in the marsh until daybreak, when he made his way to a forest.

"Travelling through the forest, he found a sharp stone, and upon that he sawed his handcuffs until they were so much worn that he snapped them across the stone, leaving one on each wrist," Troy related.[162] He then set out on a journey of one thousand miles. Often surrounded by wolves, Hutson nevertheless kept traveling until he finally made his way to Cincinnati.

By this time, Hutson no longer felt safe in Ohio. Supplied with money and clothing by the local vigilance committee, he continued northward until he reached Canada and freedom. There he was aided by Reverend Troy and other anti-slavery activists, to whom he told his remarkable tale.

Samuel May notes in *The Fugitive Slave Law and Its Victims* that near Ripley, Ohio, "a fugitive slave, about January 20 [1851], killed his pursuer. He was afterwards taken and carried back to slavery."[163] While there is no reason to doubt him, corroborating accounts have proved elusive. However, a letter by former Kentucky governor Thomas Metcalfe published in the *Daily Union* of Washington, D.C., on January 21, 1851, describes a very similar incident, which must have been the one May was referencing. It occurred in the summer of 1848.

According to Metcalfe, "An Ohioan, in pursuit of a negro from Montgomery County [Kentucky], was shot and killed by the negro."[164] Although the fugitive escaped his pursuers, he was later arrested by individuals who, though unaware of the slaying, took him across the Ohio River and lodged him in the Maysville jail.

The slave's owner allowed him to remain locked up for some time in anticipation of a requisition from the governor of Ohio, William Bebb, that he be returned to face murder charges. However, when no demand was forthcoming, he was returned to his master. A Welshman, Bebb was criticized by Welsh immigrants for his failure to fulfill his promises to them, so perhaps it's not surprising that he didn't involve himself in the fugitive slave matter.

The *Cleveland Gazette* provided an account of an incident that happened in 1851. Miss Miner (or Minor), a lady from Louisiana, and a small party of Southerners, including her uncle, stopped at the New England Hotel while passing through Cleveland. They were headed east. When some abolitionists discoved Miss Miner was accompanied by Mary Bryant, a bond servant, they obtained a writ of habeas corpus in an effort to gain the woman's freedom.

In the subsequent hearing before Judge Atkins on May 30 (which Miss Miner did not attend), the court ruled that by bringing her slave into a Free State, Miss Miner had, in effect, set her free. Told she could go where she liked, Mary chose to remain with her mistress, to whom she had tended since infancy. Judge Atkins purportedly "wasted much breath in expatiating [*sic*] to the servant on the blessings of that freedom which she did not seem to desire, and in persuading her to profit by his decision."[165] But her mind was made up.

Of course, this did not sit well with the African American citizens of Cleveland. That evening, an omnibus provided by the hotel conveyed the travelers to the wharf. As the party was about to board the *Empire State* to proceed to Buffalo, a crowd of Black men, having learned their intention, gathered about the boat. When Miss Minor and Mary Bryant were stepping on the plank, one of the men caught hold of the latter's dress and attempted to prevent her from boarding.

At this point, Deputy Marshal Clark Warren intervened. He ordered the man to desist and threatened him with a cane, permitting Mary to continue onto the ship. Another Black man, described as stout, then stepped forward and said, "You are an officer of the law, this is the law of the land, but there is a law of God."[166]

"Yes," replied Clark, "and if you don't leave this spot, you'll feel the grace of God over your head from my cane."[167] The officer drove the crowd back, allowing the Southerners to resume boarding. Mr. Miner, the uncle, tipped Warren an eagle (a gold coin worth $2.50) for his service.

The *Cleveland Herald* noted, "The *Empire State* proceeded on her way with the woman who had the good sense to prefer the guardianship of those who had been always kind, to the cold charities of those whose professions would furnish but scanty raiment, food or comfort."[168] The prospect of starting a new life, no doubt, would have been daunting to someone who had never known anything but bondage. The fact is that many former slaves were ill prepared to cope with freedom.

Chapter 8

THE RIOT IN OHIO

Writing about the Underground Railroad routes that transected Brown and Clermont Counties, William Byron described the "eastern line" as running "from Ripley by Red Oak and Russellville to Sardinia."[169] This was the spine of the abolitionist movement in Brown County, and the escape of so much valuable "property" over it was a persistent vexation to the slaveholders of Kentucky. As early as 1837, they had purportedly offered rewards of $500 to $2,500 for the capture, dead or alive, of Reverend John B. Mahon, as well as other local leaders such as Amos Pettijohn, William A. Frazier, Isaac M. Beck, John Rankin, Alexander Campbell and Williams McCoy.

According to Anne Hagedorn, the July 17, 1844 edition of the *Cincinnati Weekly Herald and Philanthropist* reported that Colonel Edward Towers, a slave owner from Mason County, Kentucky, and his men had swept in from Kentucky and administered more than one hundred lashes to Harbor Hurley, a free Black resident of Sardinia. Hurley's injuries were attested to by Dr. Isaac Morris Beck, a prominent local abolitionist. However, that was, apparently, just the prelude.

Five months later, the *Telegraph* of Georgetown, Ohio, reported that an "affray" occurred between Kentucky slave hunters and a group of abolitionists in Reverend James Gilliland's Red Oak Settlement on Monday, December 9, 1844. A handful of fugitive slaves, the property of Colonel Edward Towers of Mason, Kentucky, were being sheltered in the homes of Robert Miller and Absalom King. When Towers and his men made a search of Miller's house, two of the slaves were found. As he endeavored to help them escape, Miller was bowled over and repeatedly stabbed by the slave hunters. He bled out within seconds.

Having seized the two slaves, the Kentuckians bound them and took them to King's residence, where they expected to find the other fugitives. On arrival at the house, the raiders were met by four or five armed abolitionists, who defied them to conduct a search. Both groups began firing on one another, and the first casualty was the son of Colonel Towers. During the melee, King was shot in the back through a window as he was inside the house reloading the firearms. A Dr. Cappee was of the opinion that he could not survive his wound.

Finally, "the Sheriff, with the Georgetown Guards, and a large number of our citizens, repaired to the battle ground, to quell if possible the turbulent spirit of the rioters, and to prevent the effusion of human blood."[170] They put a quick end to the fighting and arrested the leaders of both factions. Sheriff William Shields then took the leaders to jail in Georgetown, where they would be tried before Justice Goodwin at noon the next day.

As one Pennsylvania newspaper headline declared: "In Brown county, Ohio, between Kentuckians and citizens of Ohio—Several Persons killed—Houses Burnt—Military collected to arrest the rioters!"[171] The Georgetown *Telegraph* went on to issue a call to arms: "If the Law and well-being of Society is to be thus trampled upon and sat at defiance by lawless and desperate men, it is high time for those who regard the sanctity of the law to adopt such measures as will prevent in future the recurrence of such infernal proceedings."[172]

David Gould soon arrived at the *Telegraph* office with breaking news from Red Oak: another party of Kentuckians had arrived, and more bloodshed commenced. "One of the slaves was hung without ceremony for resisting a brother of Col. Towers, who had captured him."[173] Afterward, both Miller's and King's houses were reportedly burned to the ground.

Proceeding to the home of Alexander Gilliland, the slave hunters dragged him outside and beat him nearly to death. The *Telegraph* article concluded, "The number of the Kentuckians is increasing hourly, and the whole neighborhood is up in arms. The Sheriff is actively engaged in attempting to quell the riot. Where it will end, God only knows."[174]

Famed abolitionist and social reformer William Lloyd Garrison, in the *Liberator*, was quick to react: "Here is a most bloody tragedy, enacted on free soil of Ohio, by a gang of Kentucky slave-hunters—and it is, probably, but 'the beginning of the end.'"[175] The opposition *Lexington Gazette*, on the

Many slave owners had visions of losing their property through "slave stampedes" such as this one in Virginia. *Courtesy of Library of Congress.*

other hand, asserted, "The nefarious acts of the abolitionists of Ohio in aiding and abetting the escape of our slaves are producing their natural and inevitable results—hostility and bloodshed."[176]

The Towers raid—the "Riot in Ohio"—received widespread coverage, including overseas in such publications as England's *Gentleman's Magazine* and *Spectator*. At least two men were purportedly killed (Miller and Towers' son), two others gravely wounded (King and Gilliland), two houses burned to the ground (Miller's and King's) and a Black man lynched. And at press time, the situation was expected to grow worse by the minute as additional riders from Kentucky arrived to do battle with Sheriff Shields and his martialed forces.

Six days after publishing its own account of the incident, however, the *Brooklyn Daily Eagle* admitted that it and a great many other newspapers, both in the North and the South, had been the victim of a hoax. The *New-York Daily Tribune* and the *Detroit Free Press* agreed. In fact, the *Pittsburgh Gazette* had originally delayed running the article until December 21, suspecting as much. No such incident had occurred, and "a great deal of indignation has been expended on the subject."[177]

The *Cincinnati Gazette*, which was in a position to know, explained: "It was detailed so minutely, the names were given so correctly, and the whole

Red Oak Presbyterian Church was alleged to have been the locus of a battle between Ohio abolitionists and Kentucky slave owners. *Authors' collection.*

narration had so much the appearance of reality, that we thought it was true. The motive of starting it we are at a loss to conjecture."[178] However, it was not the only instance in which newspapers were used to advance false narratives in support of or opposition to slavery. So historians must tread carefully.

In 1849, THREE SLAVES—a man, a woman and their child—escaped from the farm of a man named Harper in Boone County, Kentucky. They made their way to Cincinnati, where they were hidden away. Although Harper tried to locate them, he failed. However, he was then approached by a free Black man of the city named Keyte, who offered to buy their freedom. Keyte was thought to be the father of the male slave.

Although Harper valued the fugitives at $1,300, he agreed to sell all three to Keyte for a total of $450. Keyte gave the owner some promissory notes for the payment, underwritten by a mortgage on a piece of property he owned. But when the notes came to maturity, Harper sued Keyte for failure to pay him, seeking to foreclose on the mortgage.

In his defense, Keyte argued that he had been deceived by Harper, in that Harper had represented the enslaved female to be the wife of the enslaved male (his son) when she was not. He also charged that Harper claimed to own the male slave when, in fact, the man was not a slave at all at the time of the escape because he had driven a wagon to Cincinnati on behalf of his master. Under some interpretations of the law, he would have gained his freedom as soon as he entered Ohio. And finally, he maintained that a contract for the purchase of fugitive slaves undertaken in the State of Ohio was not legally tenable.

In a decision handed down on July 26, 1851, Judge Key ruled first that the relationship between the male and female slaves was supported by the facts and that she was properly described as his wife in the prevailing usage of the term among slaves. Second, while the slave could have asserted his freedom when he drove the wagon to Cincinnati, he did not do so but voluntarily returned to Kentucky. And third, the United States Supreme Court had already decided in a case involving the same question that the status of an alleged fugitive from slavery was governed by the law of the state from which he escaped.

Since Harper had the right of recapture, that was enough to sustain a contract of sale executed in a Free State, although not all would agree. Therefore, Harper was entitled to foreclose on Keyte's "property."

William Lloyd Garrison, abolitionist and editor of the *Liberator*, was outraged by the purported riot at Red Oak incident. *Courtesy Library of Congress.*

FOLLOWING THE PASSAGE OF the Fugitive Slave Act, so-called slave stampedes were reported with increasing frequency. In September 1852, thirty slaves "vamoosed" from Maysville, Kentucky, to Ripley, Ohio. "Trouble is expected," newspapers reported.[179] Clearly, tension was building between the two states. On the evening of October 20, 1852, a party of seven fugitive slaves (two men, two women and three children) arrived in Sandusky from Kentucky aboard the Mad River & Lake Erie Railroad. Their friends immediately conveyed them to the steamer *Arrow*, which was about to embark for Detroit. But they were apprehended by three slave hunters from Kentucky just as the vessel was casting off from the Mad River Dock.

"Three of the slaves were claimed by one Lewis F. Weimer," Rush Sloane later wrote, "and four by Charles M. Gibbons."[180] According to the *Sandusky Mirror*, one of the Kentuckians had "seized hold of a young woman with an infant, eight or nine months old, in her arms."[181] Wrenching herself free, the woman ran several steps, dropped the child to the ground and then returned to confront her assailant. She was promptly arrested, while the child was picked up by a local citizen.

Although one slave hunter claimed the baby was his, the citizen refused to surrender it without proof. When the infant was taken to the mother, she denied it was hers, fearing that it would be returned to slavery along with her. "The citizens were told by the marshal [O. Rice], as he flourished his cane, that it was a legal arrest and that the fugitives would be discharged unless the mayor should so decide."[182]

The *Sandusky Register* reported that "the woman and her children were forcibly dragged on shore and taken directly to the office of F.N. Follet, Mayor, by an individual claiming them."[183] Almost immediately, numerous spectators poured into the mayor's office, among them more than twenty African Americans. The angry throng, many brandishing clubs, pistols and knives, created an atmosphere that was both tense and chaotic.

Attorney Sloane, hired by the city's people of color to represent the fugitives, waited for half an hour for the claimant to identify himself. Finally, he asked if Marshall Rice was in the room, and after a delay, Rice stepped forward. Described by the newspaper as "a coarse, ignorant, well-meaning man," he had apparently assisted the slavecatchers.[184]

Asked if the slaves were in his custody, Rice replied that they weren't. When Sloane then asked if they were in the custody of any United States official within the room, there was no response. Therefore, he demanded that the arrest warrants be produced. At this point, Rice admitted there

In truth, there was no "riot" in Ohio; no one was killed, and no property was destroyed. *Courtesy New York Public Library.*

were none—nor was there any other paperwork. Clearly, the enslaved had not been arrested by a U.S. marshal or deputy marshal as required by law.

"Then, my friends," said Mr. Sloane, speaking with deliberate calmness, "there is nothing in the world to hinder you from going when and where you please."[185]

At this, John B. Lott, an African American gentleman, "cried out in an excited voice, 'Hustle them out.'"[186] In the ensuing confusion, the crowd rushed as a body out of the court room, apparently with the woman and her children. As they did, one of the Kentuckians who had been standing near Sloane the entire time said he was their owner. He then turned to Rice and said, "I gave you the papers once, and will hold you, too, responsible, for you might have stopped them."[187]

Alternatively, the man handed the papers to Sloane and said, "I own the Negroes. I'll hold you individually responsible for their escape."[188] To which Sloane purportedly replied that he was "good for them."

By the time the slaves' owner presented his papers of ownership, the fugitives had been placed aboard a small vessel by their friends. They were later transferred to a larger vessel, in which they safely landed in Canada. However, the owner then filed charges against Sloane under the Fugitive

Slave Act. Tried in the U.S. District Court in Columbus, the attorney was fined $3,000 plus another $1,330.30 in court and legal fees. Meanwhile, the citizens of Sandusky were charged with "a want of disposition to execute the law."[189]

Although states' rights—the political powers held by state governments—remain an issue today, they were at the forefront of the struggle over slavery. The Bill of Rights was specifically created because Massachusetts refused to ratify the U.S. Constitution without it. And if the prohibition on slavery had not been eliminated, there would have been no United States of America.

The autonomy of the individual slave states was repeatedly upheld in various courts around the country. Take the case of Sarah Haynes (also known as Sarah Mielke). She was formerly owned by Edward C. Mielke of Vicksburg, Mississippi, who passed away in 1846. Three years earlier, in April 1843, Sarah left his service for Cincinnati, bearing the following permit issued by her master: "My negro woman, Sarah Haynes, about thirty years old, has permission to pass unmolested to Cincinnati and the State of Ohio generally, or any other free State she may choose."[190]

Mielke purportedly paid Sarah's passage to Ohio with the intent of setting her free under the principle of "automatic freedom": that is, she would become free by stepping foot in a Free State. A few days later, she left Ohio for New Orleans, where she established her residence.

However, in 1853, the Supreme Court of Louisiana ruled that Sarah had violated the law by coming into the state and remaining there. The court did not recognize that she had attained her freedom simply by going to Cincinnati. The court ruled that "her status must be determined according to the laws of the domicil [sic] of her master": that is, Mississippi.[191] Therefore, she was enslaved once again.

A slave owner's intent with respect to his slaves' freedom was becoming a thorny issue in the country's courts, as it was in the case of Henrietta Wood. "Six feet tall, of commanding presence," she was born in Boone County, Kentucky, according to newspaper accounts.[192] She was the property of Mrs. Jane Cirode of Louisville, Kentucky.

On removing to Cincinnati in 1847, Cirode executed a deed of manumission and gave it to Wood; then they parted company. But when

Cirode passed away some years later, her children decided that Wood should be included as part of their mother's estate, claiming that Cirode had no right to sell Wood because she did not have full legal ownership of her.

In April 1853, Mrs. Rebecca Boyd, who purportedly had known Jane Cirode, induced Wood to climb into a buggy in Cincinnati. Then, assisted by Frank Rust, her boarder, and John Gilbert, a Black man, she hurried her across the Ohio River to Covington, Kentucky. Once there, they delivered Wood to Zebulon "Zeb" Ward, sheriff of Campbell County, who had purchased the woman from Cirode's heirs for $300—some $700 below her estimated value.

Boyd, Rust and Gilbert were subsequently tried and acquitted of kidnapping in Cincinnati. While still being held by Ward, Henrietta Wood tried to regain her freedom by filing a petition in the Fayette County circuit court. However, in January 1854, the court ruled that she had no standing to sue because she was a slave.

After keeping Wood in "duress seven month[s]," the sheriff sold her to a Frankfort slave trader named William Pullian, who took her to Mississippi and sold her to Gerard Brandon, a cotton planter, for $1,050. For the next fifteen years, Wood remained a slave, working mostly in Mississippi and then Texas as the Union army made its way toward Vicksburg.

Although Wood should have been freed by the Emancipation Proclamation on January 1, 1863, she was kept in bondage for five more years. Owing to this delay, she was prevented from returning home to Cincinnati until 1869. Then, with the support of her friends, she sued Zebulon Ward for $15,000 (or possibly $20,000) for duress and abduction. By this time, he was a prosperous citizen of Little Rock, Arkansas.

In his defense, Ward claimed he had purchased Wood from Robert White and others who claimed to be her owners. However, the court was not convinced and ordered him to pay $2,500 and costs. As one newspaper noted, "The sum mentioned seems a trifling recompense for the 15 years of bondage."[193]

Chapter 9

HIDING PLACES

Any structure of sufficient age (and a few that aren't) is apt to be touted as an Underground Railroad station, safe house or depot: that is, a hiding place. Proving it, however, is another matter. Fugitive slaves sometimes found refuge in private homes, barns, schoolhouses, churches, taverns, offices and even caves. Some of these were used more than once. Others were spur-of-the-moment accommodations. Relatively few were identified as such at the time because that would have opened up those who were aiding and abetting the fugitives to criminal prosecution, although a few, such as John Rankin, obviously didn't care. So it was only later—much later—that people began making such claims.

More than a century and a half after the Civil War ended, real estate agents and preservationists discovered that an old house that once harbored runaway slaves was more valuable than a similar old house that didn't. As a consequence, the number of "UGRR houses" has exploded. Proof of these claims is often quite elusive, based primarily on oral history, local legend or wishful thinking. In some instances, the homes weren't built until later, or their owners were anything but against slavery.

More recently, some of these alleged UGRR houses have also been said to be "haunted" by ghostly spirits—an even more dubious claim. To quote naturalist John Burroughs, "The ghost story gives a new interest to the old house."[194] Incredibly, a number of university presses have published books about such purported hauntings. In doing so, they have generally set aside all pretense of academic rigor. Even the history is suspect and frequently unsourced. Nonetheless, books of this sort often sell better than serious histories.

Tourism is a tough business; it's a zero-sum game. Travelers have only so much disposable income and free time to spend traveling. It is imperative that hotels, museums and towns find a way to stand out from the competition and attract visitors. Historical preservation is an equally difficult enterprise. It is financially impossible and impractical to save every building, and frankly, just because a building is old doesn't mean it's significant. So what is the owner of a historic home to do? If they're clever and don't mind lying, they could do what many places have done and make up a ghost story—the bloodier the better.

The Myrtles Plantation in Louisiana bills itself as "one of America's most haunted homes," with at least a dozen ghosts.[195] It also is purportedly the site of ten murders. In support of this claim, the owners have gone so far as to invent enslaved people who never existed and then brutally kill them off in murders that never happened. Although the original fiction has been softened by deeming it a "legend," the plantation's website encourages potential customers to book a tour in order to learn the truth about the

Columbus's Kelton House has a very well-documented UGRR story, complete with letters and photographs. *Courtesy of MJ/Wikipedia.*

Originally from Vermont, Fernando Cortez Kelton was a prominent dry goods merchant. *Courtesy Kelton House.*

many homicides alleged to have taken place there. To reinforce the ghost angle, it includes a spirit photo of one of the ghosts: Chloe.

Troy Taylor, author of the Haunted America supernatural history series, thoroughly discredited the Chloe legend on his website through the use of publicly available records.[196] In fact, Chloe is not listed in the records of all the enslaved persons owned by the Woodruff family, the original plantation owners. Therefore, the consensus among historians is that Chloe never existed and the multiple murders, including hers, never occurred.

There are more than a few purported UGRR houses in Ohio that are said to be haunted—and the reason is economics. Ghost tourism is big business. Many people prefer fake history to the real thing. They are seeking thrills, not edification. Old buildings provide them with a sort of theater in which they can allow their imaginations to run wild, without fear of any real danger. The Ohio State Reformatory in Mansfield, the former Ohio State Insane Asylum in Athens and Prospect Place in Dresden are touted by reality TV as among the most haunted places in the United States. But it seems especially disrespectful to exploit the national tragedy of slavery in such a callous manner—to fabricate sensational stories out of whole cloth.

KELTON HOUSE IN COLUMBUS, Ohio, supposedly has a ghost or two, but hauntings are not a featured attraction—except during Halloween season. A Victorian Greek Revival home, it was built by Fernando Cortez Kelton in 1852. Both he and his wife, Sophia, hailed from Vermont. They were members of the local anti-slavery society and, evidently, supporters of the Underground Railroad to some extent. This can be said with a high degree of certainty because the name and history of one of the fugitives they took in is known. There is even a photograph.

In 1864, a year after the UGRR is generally thought to have ceased operations, Sophia discovered a young Black girl hiding in her yard. The girl, Martha Hartway, was born a slave in Powhattan County, Virginia, in September 1854 (or 1858). At the age of ten, Martha and her sister, Pearl, purportedly fled the plantation at their mother's urging. When Mrs. Kelton found them concealed under a bush beside her home, Martha was too ill to move. However, Pearl continued on to Wisconsin.

For the next ten years, Martha remained with the Kelton family. Then, in 1874, she married Thomas Lawrence in the front parlor of the house. The son of free Blacks, Thomas worked for the Keltons as a cabinetmaker. Martha and her husband continued to reside with the Keltons until they could obtain their own house.

Fortunately, the story does not end there. In the late 1960s, an African America woman, Ruth Lawrence, began to wonder why her late mother-in-law held onto some old photos of White people. This eventually led her to Columbus and the Kelton House and resulted in two years of research by Beverly M. Gordon of Ohio State University.

The photos had the name "Kelton" written on many of them. Ruth's late father-in-law and late brother-in-law name were both named Arthur Kelton Lawrence, but the Lawrences were Black. So Ruth asked her husband if they were his relatives. He didn't know. Finally, she called Grace Kelton, the last member of the family to live in the house at 586 East Town Street. Grace responded, "Oh, I had wondered what became of that family."[197] In her nineties by then, Grace invited Ruth to visit and showed her the woodwork that her husband's grandfather Thomas Lawrence had crafted during the thirty years he worked for the family.

Years later, Gordon obtained a grant to further research the history of Thomas Lawrence and Martha Hartway. She believes that the young girl traveled to Columbus from Virginia at the behest of her older brother, Julius Aurelius Hartway. He had come to Ohio earlier. "We do not know under what circumstances or conditions that John Hartway left his sister Martha with the Keltons," she noted.[198]

Thomas Lawrence, a free Black man born in Cadiz, Ohio, arrived in Columbus in 1872 and soon went to work for the Keltons. The marriage of Martha and Thomas clearly had the Keltons' approval. Their son, Arthur Kelton Lawrence, would graduate from the Ohio State University College of Pharmacy, possibly the first Black student to do so. And after serving in the Spanish-American War, he obtained a degree in medicine, also from Ohio State.

The progress exhibited by the Lawrence family, Beverly concluded, illustrated that "despite all the racial tension, the racial strife of that era,

Left: Sophia Kelton, alongside her husband, was a fervent abolitionist. *Courtesy Kelton House.*

Right: In 1864, Sophia discovered Martha Hartway (pictured) hiding in her yard. *Courtesy Kelton House.*

there were progressively minded whites who were supportive. They realized that the black community was not asking for handouts."[199]

According to oral tradition, other runaways were hidden in the barn behind the house, in a three-hundred-gallon cistern in the washhouse or even in the servants' quarters on the third floor. However, Susie Harpham, former chairman of the Kelton Property Commission, believed that the Kelton house handled only the overflow. She thought "the primary destination of runaway slaves was 530 E. Town St....which actually had a secret room in which to hide slaves."[200] This was the Snowden-Gray Mansion, now a private event venue. The home was built in 1852–54 by Philip T. Snowden and his wife, Abigail. However, hard evidence of UGRR activity is lacking.

Early in 1848, John D. Brown died. A slaveholder from Henrico, Virginia, Brown owned a substantial number of slaves (thirty at the time of his death) distributed among three family groups, not counting his own. One of his slaves, Caroline, was "his woman" (although he also referred to her as his "indentured servant"), and presumably, Edward and Constantia, her children, were his children as well. In the *Henrico County (Va.) Registers of Free Negroes, 1831–1865*, Caroline was described as "a woman of a light brown complexion."[201] Edward and Constantia were said to be even lighter than their mother.

The relationship between a slave owner and an enslaved person can never been construed as a love story given the inherently unequal power dynamic between them. However, Caroline and her children were accorded special treatment in John D. Brown's will. Not only did Caroline inherit a curtained bedstead, which was remarkable in itself, but all three of them were also given their freedom and the proceeds from the sale of his estate so that they could relocate to Ohio.[202] The estate consisted largely of the twenty-seven other slaves, who were auctioned off. It's likely that most if not all the owner's wealth was invested in his slaves.

For some reason, Caroline, Edward and Constantia did not immediately leave Virginia, possibly because it took several years to settle the estate. No doubt there were outstanding debts paid. Consequently, they were still listed in Virginia's *Register of Free Negroes* in 1851. Per John's will, Edward was to receive two-thirds of monies derived from the sale of the estate so that he could "support and maintain his mother, Caroline, for and during her natural life," and the other third was to go to Constantia. Since Edward was illiterate, two executors, James S. Ryall and Samuel Davis, were charged with purchasing land in Ohio, which they then deeded over to Edward.

It is believed that Caroline, Edward and Constantia arrived in Columbus around 1852. Caroline was said to be nearing seventy, while her two children seem to have been about twenty-one or twenty-two years old. The original home was not the beautiful Greek Revival dwelling that now stands at the corner of Livingston and Linwood Avenues, but a more modest four-room structure with a flat roof.[203] A second floor was later added.

Caroline purportedly died in 1869, and Edward sold the house to an Asa Parker in 1877. Census records suggest that both Edward and Constantia passed for White once they moved to Ohio, with Constantia marrying a Danish immigrant, John Johnson, and Edward

Thomas Lawrence married Martha Hartway (pictured) ten years after she met the Keltons. *Courtesy Kelton House.*

taking up residence with a Sorg family from Württemberg, Germany, as early as 1870.

More than a century later, rumors began to circulate that the Browns had harbored fugitives from slavery in their home. Furthermore, some claimed there were tunnels that led from the house to a nearby barn and ended near Main Street. However, no source for this information is given by those making the claim, so the Browns' involvement in the Underground Railroad cannot be substantiated.

On Friday, July 8, 1853, a party of men—three from Kentucky, including a slave owner named Ed Pierce (or Pearce), and two from Ohio—passed through the village of New Petersburg in Highland County. They were in pursuit of three fugitives, two men and a woman, who had escaped from Mason and Fleming Counties in Kentucky the previous Sunday. They believed the freedom seekers were headed toward Greenfield but had not yet reached Rattlesnake Creek.

Alarmed by the presence of slave hunters in their community, many citizens of New Petersburg suddenly found themselves aligned with the anti-slavery cause. One prominent gentleman went so far as to ask the men to produce a warrant for the slaves. Instead, one of them drew a revolver and replied, "That was the only warrant they needed."[204]

Since two roads led to Greenfield, both of which crossed the creek, three of the slave hunters stationed themselves at the bridge and two at the ford about half a mile away, near Rainsboro. As the *Ohio Star* reported:

> *The party at the bridge had not waited long, when the slaves, two men and a woman, made their appearance, escorted by a white man and a boy as guides. As soon as they were fairly within the bridge, which is a covered one the Kentuckians sprang upon them, and a desperate fight ensued.*[205]

The White man was known as Sumner; the boy was not identified.

Armed with "guns, pistols and knives," the slaves put up a desperate fight. Gunfire was exchanged, and two of them, including a man owned by a slaveholder named McDowell and the young woman owned by Pierce, were known to have been hit, but they managed to escape. In the struggle, Pierce was nearly choked to death.

The second Black man, the property of an owner named Dobyns who lived near Lewisburg, Kentucky, suffered a deep cut. He was captured and taken to jail in Maysville, Kentucky. Sumner "was also caught and beaten in a very severe manner with a club," according to one account, "and strong hopes are entertained that he will die."[206]

In their wake, the slaves left behind the broken breach of a gun, a pistol and a considerable amount of blood. The slave hunters tracked the fugitives about a mile and a half by their blood trail but did not overtake them, so they returned home without their captive.

SOME ENSLAVED PEOPLE PROVED to be masters of disguise. Jackson, likely named after President Andrew Jackson, was the slave of William R. King, president of the United States Senate and vice president under President Franklin Pierce.[207] King, a native of Alabama, and his relatives owned more than five hundred slaves altogether.

While his master was in Washington, D.C., Jackson ran away to Cincinnati, where he operated a barbershop for several years. But King eventually learned of his whereabouts and sent his agent to recapture him. Because the agent did not have the required writ, he planned to take Jackson by force. Accompanied by a posse of armed men, the agent jumped Jackson as he was headed to dinner and dragged him down to the wharf, where a ferry was waiting.

With no legal recourse, Jackson was "bound and carried back to Alabama, where he remained in slavery two or three years, and where he married a free woman, a Creole, of Mobile, who possessed some property."[208] She was the daughter of William King's brother by a favorite slave and had been brought up with his other children. According to Jackson's wife, her father had freed her before his death but left no documentation.

Because Jackson's wife could pass as an "elegant Southern lady," they hatched a plan to travel north with him pretending to be her servant. Departing from New Orleans, they headed upriver to Cincinnati. Along the way, she was warned by other Southern ladies on board that if they disembarked in Cincinnati, she would risk losing her slave, but she told them she was not concerned. On the other hand, the Northern ladies told Jackson that he should take the opportunity to escape when they reached Ohio, but he insisted he wasn't interested.

On the morning of January 18, 1853, a couple of fugitive slaves arrived in Cincinnati from Alabama. As reported in the *Liberator*, "The husband being quite dark and of small stature, was diguised in female apparel, and passed as the servant for his wife, who is white, and withal very beautiful."[209] When they disembarked in Cincinnati, the couple took a carriage to Dumas House, a public hotel operated by a Black man.

Within a few hours, Levi Coffin, the so-called president of the Underground Railroad, was summoned to the hotel, accompanied by John Hatfield, an African American who was also active in the UGRR. It was there that Coffin met "a fine-looking, well-dressed Creole, with straight black hair and olive complexion."[210] He also met her servant, "Sal"—that is, her husband dressed in women's clothing. Although both Coffin and Hatfield knew Jackson from when he was living in Cincinnati, neither of them recognized him until he removed his disguise.

Because Jackson was so well known in Cincinnati, Coffin and Hatfield did not feel it was safe for him to remain there. Instead, he would go to Cleveland by train the following night. Once he was settled, he would send for his wife. Much like he had in Cincinnati, Jackson opened a barbershop in Cleveland, and he and his wife decided to make the city their home.

Chapter 10

THE GREAT BEAR

For many years, schoolchildren have been taught that "Follow the Drinking Gourd" was an African American folksong that provided freedom seekers with instructions for how to make their way north along the Underground Railroad. In fact, it might be called the UGRR's unofficial song. No doubt it has helped bring the history alive. But is it true?

The Drinking Gourd was another name for the Big Dipper, a pattern of stars in the night sky located in the constellation Ursa Major, or the Greater Bear. According to historian Joel Bresler, the song was first "collected" by amateur folklorist H.B. Parks, who purportedly heard it being sung by a Black youth in the mountains of Hot Springs, North Carolina, in 1912.

A year later, Parks claimed he heard a Black fisherman "singing the same stanza of the same tune" on the wharf in Louisville, Kentucky.[211] Then, in 1918, he said he heard two Black children singing the same tune at the train depot in Waller, Texas, but the lyrics were "Foller the Risen Lawd."[212] What's more, over the next decade, Parks purportedly met an "old negro at College Station, Texas," who explained the meaning of the song to him.

It's an incredible story, to be sure. Parks heard this previously unknown song from three different sources in three widely dispersed locales spanning nearly one hundred thousand square miles and then met someone who could explain it to him. Finally, Parks said, he was able to confirm it with his great-uncle—also quite a coincidence or, more likely, a string of falsehoods.

According to Parks, a man known as "Peg Leg" Joe worked on the UGRR north of Mobile, Alabama. He moved from plantation to plantation as a

The Big Dipper, also known as the Plow, is just a small part of the constellation Ursa Major, the Great Bear. *Courtesy of Library of Congress.*

journeyman laborer. But his mission was to teach the "Drinking Gourd" song to slaves so they could use it to make their escape. The lyrics of the song included coded references to the geography of Alabama. But there is no proof that Joe ever existed. Furthermore, the song was never collected in Alabama.

Parks first published "Drinking Gourd" in 1928, under the sponsorship of the Texas Folklore Society. It was subsequently reprinted in 1934 by John A. and Alan Lomax in *American Ballads and Folksongs*. A different, more polished version of the song later appeared in *People's Songs*. It was attributed to folk singer Lee Hays, "who as a child heard it this way [melody only] from his nurse, Aunty Laura," in Forrest City, Arkansas, sometime during 1916 to 1920.[213] However, Hays never said anything about Aunty Laura to his biographer, Doris Willens, who considered him a "fabulist"—a person who makes up elaborate stories.

In 1932, Mary Hunter Austin mentioned the song in her autobiography, *Earth Horizon*. She claimed that she heard Moses Drakeford, the only African American man in town, sing "Foller d drinkin'-gou'd" in Carlinville, Illinois, when she was five or six years old. This would have been around 1873. It turns out there was a Black man named Moses Drakeford, a farm laborer,

The banjo evolved out of an African instrument and played a prominent role in the music of enslaved people. *Authors' collection.*

living in Carlinville during this period. He passed away in 1924, before "Drinking Gourd" was published. Amazingly, Carlinville happened to be the hometown of H.B. Parks, too. This raises the possibility that Parks heard the song from Drakeford and then lied about its source for some reason.

The coded geographical references in "Follow the Drinking Gourd" make this "map song"—a song used to teach geography—an anomaly among all folk songs and also tie it to a very specific locale. The cryptic directions would have been worthless to anyone who wasn't escaping from a certain point in Alabama. And successful escapes from the Deep South were rare. Actually, many fugitives from slavery in the lower Southern states remained there or went west. So the "Drinking Gourd" seems more like a folktale that was turned into a song years later. But it's still a good song, and Parks was either the writer or stole it from someone else.

In order to gain Black people's confidence, slave catchers often claimed to be their friends, in much the same way that Quakers were known as Friends. But it was just another trick.

About noon on May 25, 1854, Eli Cook, a middle-aged African American man of "respectable appearance," was hiking alone on the Columbus and Xenia Turnpike near Cedarville when David McCord overtook him in a buggy.[214] Claiming to be a "friend to the colored man," McCord invited Cook to ride along with him.[215] Cook accepted his offer.

Since they were traveling through abolitionist territory, McCord proposed that Cook "represent himself as a fugitive slave"; McCord would pretend to be an agent or conductor of the UGRR.[216] In this way, they might be able to obtain donations from any opponents of slavery they might encounter along the way. However, this enterprise did not meet with much success.

According to the *National Era*, "The only person they met was a lapsed disciple of George Fox [founder of the Quakers], who replied to their story, that gold and silver he had none, but such as he had they were welcome to—pulling out a bottle of whiskey and treating them."[217]

Taking the Jamestown Road, the two men continued on until they reached the home of William Chapman and his son, John (some accounts reverse their names), "three miles south of Selma, in Greene county."[218] McCord asked the elder Chapman if there were any abolitionists or Quakers residing on that road. He replied there were none that he knew of. He also informed McCord that his family was from Virginia and he had no sympathy for runaway slaves.

Stepping down from the buggy, McCord walked past William, who was standing at the gate, and continued on to the house. William followed him, and they briefly conversed on the porch. They then walked back to the buggy, and McCord instructed Cook to drive up to the gate. After unhitching the horse, he told the Black man to go into the house.

While John took the horse to the stable, the three men went into the kitchen. On his return, he saw McCord struggling with the Black man, whose head was bleeding. At this point, John tried to intervene, but Cook fell to the floor, and McCord fell with him. Turning Cook on his face, McCord directed John to help him tie the man up. John started to fashion a noose out of a strap, which McCord handed to him.

John had not completed this task when McCord struck Cook on the head with a Colt pistol. As they bound the man, McCord told John that Cook was "a fugitive slave, that there was a reward offered for his arrest and return—that he knew his master, and that if I would assist him to take [the Black man] to Cincinnati, I should have half the reward [$200]."[219]

Although John said he initially refused McCord's offer, he eventually took him up on it because he believed the law made it his duty to assist in the return of fugitive slaves. He then went to a neighbor's house to borrow a pistol for his own protection. When John returned, he saw Cook running down the road. He had somehow managed to free himself.

McCord ran after him, crying, "Catch the damned horse thief," with William Chapman and his son trailing behind him.[220] When the fugitive picked up a stone, McCord swung a club, striking him on the head. He then bound him once more and forced him to walk to the buggy, assisted by McCord and John Chapman.

As they set off down the road, John realized that Cook was failing quickly. They had not gone more than two or three miles before McCord turned off into David Wilson's woods. However, he spotted a man there and quickly returned to the road. After driving another three miles, they saw a carriage coming toward them and pulled off into a wood until it had passed.

Once again, they returned to the road. By this time, Cook appeared to be near death. They continued on until they were a mile or two beyond the village of Clifton. Driving the buggy into a wood on the south side of the road, they lifted Cook, who seemed to be dead, and placed him "in a sitting posture against a tree."[221]

Cook's beating and subsequent removal in the buggy had been observed by some of the Chapmans' neighbors. Newspapers reported that "these facts came to the ears of Daniel P. Wilson and Joseph Laird, who disguised themselves as slave hunters and appeared at Chapman's in the night."[222] The two men learned enough of the details from the younger Chapman to justify a charge of kidnapping against father and son. The following morning, the Chapmans were arrested and bound over to the court to face charges for the crime. Wilson and Laird began pressuring John Chapman to tell them what had become of the Black man. Although John initially tried to deceive them, he eventually led them to where they had left the body.

The enslaved sang work songs, spirituals, popular tunes and songs both comic and sorrowful. *Authors' collection.*

News of the murder created quite a stir in the neighborhood, and a local man named Samuel Howard (or perhaps Howell) decided to search for McCord in Xenia. He learned that on Friday evening, the day after the murder, McCord had left for Spring Valley. Consequently, Howard offered a fifty-dollar reward for McCord's apprehension, and McCord was taken "with some difficulty" the next day.[223] He was brought back to Xenia and locked in the local jail.

After Cook's body was discovered, Coroner J.W. Manor was sent for, and an inquest was held. John Chapman, as the key witness, described how McCord had come to his father's house with a "colored man." When McCord asked them whether they would like to help him purchase Cook's freedom, his father replied, "No! He would rather help him back into slavery."[224] McCord then instructed John to feed his horse.

While the son was taking the horse to the stable, his father, McCord and the Black man went into the kitchen. Not long afterward, the younger Chapman's sister came running out of the house, crying that they were killing a man inside.

Entering the house, John Chapman found McCord and the Black man falling to the floor; the latter's head was bleeding. McCord fetched a hitching strap and asked John to restrain the Black man. He then struck Cook over the head with a Colt pistol, grasping him around the throat with his other hand. After binding the Black man's hands behind him, the men put him in another room. However, while John was off borrowing a gun from a neighbor, the Black man got loose and attempted to escape— leading to his death.

The *Herald of Freedom* reported, "Chapman's testimony was given in such a manner as to show that he was falsifying, and part of the facts were drawn from him by involving him in contradictions."[225] Certainly,

Suggestions that some songs imparted secret messages to aid fugitives, such as this one, in their flight are unsubstantiated. *Authors' collection.*

newspaper reporters seemed to be confused and had difficulty getting the Chapmans' names right. Doctors Butler and Newell of Clifton certified that Cook's death was caused by the beating he sustained. The suspects said they believed they were killing a horse thief, although their own testimony contradicted this.

The coroner's jury ruled that "the deceased came to his death by blows from a colt and club in the hands of one William McCord, assisted by the two Chapmans."[226] John testified that McCord proposed he join him in the kidnapping business and said he knew where they could quickly find four more victims.

Following a hearing before Justice of the Peace T. Marshall, the Chapmans, having confessed to their involvement, were released on $1,000 bail. It was thought they would leave the country. But the *Xenia Torchlight* reported they were soon rearrested and had a hearing before Esquire Currie of Cedarville.

On December 1, 1854, McCord, who could not come up with the $1,000 bail money, was convicted of murder in the second degree and sentenced to the Ohio Penitentiary for life. He was defended by Messrs. Scott Vallandigham and his father, Clement—the famous "Copperhead" (a.k.a. Peace Democrat)—who argued that the evidence would only support a verdict of manslaughter. Judge Rodgers said he would have been satisfied with that, but he did not want to overrule the jury. In time, it was learned that the victim, Cook, had been a free man who lived near Waynesville in Warren County with his wife and two children.

FREEDOM SEEKERS HARVEY AND his son, George, were discovered in Cincinnati after escaping from their master, Henry Sumptall (or perhaps Tunstall) of Jefferson County, Kentucky. An earlier attempt had been made to capture them near Cumminsville, a settlement on the edge of Cincinnati. The two of them were assisted in their escape by "a black rascal of the name of Jesse Smith, alias Shakespeare," who gave them a ride in his baggage wagon. Henry was said to have purchased "fine clothes," only to have them stolen from him by his abolitionist friends.[227]

George was apprehended at College Hill. The two had apparently been in hiding at a gentleman's house in Cincinnati for several days before venturing out again. However, as a newspaper reported, "Harvey, the father, took to the woods and escaped, and it was supposed that he had fled to Canada by the underground railroad."[228] He was purportedly carrying "plenty of money."[229]

Then, late in September 1854, Harvey was arrested near Goshen, Ohio. He had been hiding out in a house in Newtown, about ten miles from Cincinnati. "One Wednesday [September 20] one of the colored pretended friends gave information to the officers who suddenly visited the house on Wednesday evening, and arrested him and brought him to" Cincinnati, where he was lodged in the Hamilton County jail.[230]

On September 22, 1854, U.S. Commissioner John L. Pendery examined Harvey and remanded him back to his owner. His arrest had greatly agitated the African Americans living in Cincinnati.

SLAVE CATCHING AS AN occupation was not without peril. Although Kentucky was a slave state, not all Kentuckians supported those who hunted slaves, especially when they did so in an indiscriminate fashion. The issue came to a head in Maysville, Kentucky, in November 1854.

Sometime during the first week of November, "three worthless fellows named Young" forced their way into a house in Georgetown, Ohio, around midnight.[231] Masquerading as officers of the law, they abducted a young Black woman and carried her back to Maysville, where they planned to sell her into slavery. However, they were followed "by four negro men, one of whom crossed over to Maysville and gave information of the outrage."[232]

After being hidden away for a couple of days, the unidentified woman was able to escape from her place of confinement. She then "gave information which led to the arrest [on November 10] of three brothers, named Henry, Lewis, and Allen Young, who were committed to jail to await trial."[233] They admitted they made their living by stealing and selling people of color, whether free or bound.

The Young brothers were well known in the community, having grown up there. Furthermore, their father was a "highly respectable gentleman of the neighborhood."[234] Two of them still lived in Maysville, while the third made his home in Ohio, where he apparently scouted for likely victims.

Nevertheless, the citizens of Maysville were incensed by the presence of "consummate scoundrels" in their town. Three days later, they held a large meeting at the courthouse to devise a plan for dealing with them. Forming a procession, they escorted the Young brothers "across the Ohio River, and delivered them into the hands of the officers of the law, to be dealt with and punished for the offense of kidnapping."[235]

"There was no tumultuous violence in the act, but a quiet determination which neither officers nor the law of our State attempted to interrupt," according to the *Maysville Express*. "It was the act of slaveholders proclaiming to the world their determination to deal justly, despite the wrongs so often done to their rights."[236]

A letter in the *Frankfort Yeoman* further defined the problem: "Kidnapping free negroes in Ohio, and deluding our slaves from their masters to recapture and sell them, is an established profession of a gang located upon the borders of the Ohio, combining with negro traders in the interior of this State."[237]

But the story doesn't end there. Years later, historian J. Winston Coleman wrote that when the police became involved, "these men threatened to burn the town if the police insisted on making further investigations, and it was necessary to appoint vigilance committees to extinguish numerous fires. During this melee a number of Maysville slaves were spirited away to the central Kentucky market and eventually to the South."[238]

Chapter 11

EVERYONE'S DARLING

D arling Nelly Gray," composed by Ohio songwriter Benjamin R. Hanby, has been called the *Uncle Tom's Cabin* of popular song. But unlike Harriet Beecher Stowe's six-hundred-page novel, which must be read from cover to cover to be fully appreciated, Hanby's five succinct verses and a chorus can be sung in under five minutes. "A song leaps from heart to heart," as Ohio Congressman Clarence Brown stated on reading the lyrics into the congressional record.[239]

Not only was "Nellie Gray" frequently sung by Union soldiers around their campfires, but it was also second only to "Dixie" (also by an Ohioan, Daniel Emmett of Mount Vernon) in popularity among Confederate soldiers. As Ohio historian Charles B. Galbreath wrote in 1906, "No song has been more widely sung and responsively heard by a whole nation than 'Darling Nelly Gray,' the plaintive war-time ballad which still remains familiar to thousands of ears on both sides of the obliterated Mason and Dixon's line."[240]

Hanby purportedly wrote "Darling Nelly Gray" in 1856 while attending Otterbein University in Westerville, Ohio. His inspiration was his family's involvement with Joseph Selby, a fugitive slave from Kentucky, whom the Hanbys had taken into their Rushville, Ohio home in 1842, when Benjamin was nine. Benjamin's father was Reverend William Hanby, a minister of the United Brethren Church and a conductor of the Underground Railroad.

By the time Selby found his way to Rushville, he was both physically ill and heartsick. Before he succumbed to pneumonia, he told the Hanbys that when he fled Kentucky, he had to leave behind his girlfriend, Nelly Gray,

"Darling Nelly Gray," published in 1856, was inspired by a true incident Benjamin Hanby heard about while in college. *Authors' collection.*

who had been sold to a master in Georgia. His hope was to raise money to purchase her freedom. However, before Reverend Hanby could help him do so, Selby died. He was subsequently buried in a corner of the Rushville cemetery, which would also come to hold the remains of four other fugitives from slavery. "It was while standing at these graves that young Hanby heard

Nelly, the sweetheart of Joe Selby, was sold to a slave owner in Georgia; he would never see her again. *Authors' collection.*

the story of Joe Selby, the slave, as learned from his father," according to a newspaper account at the time.[241]

George E. Kalb, a longtime Rushville resident, would claim many years later that Benjamin actually wrote the first draft of the song at his grandmother's house in the autumn of 1855, while he was teaching school in Rushville. On returning to Westerville at the end of the term, Hanby revised the song. To support his claim, Kalb produced two additional verses that were omitted from the revised version.[242] The budding songwriter would also pen several other anti-slavery songs, as well as the popular Christmas song "Up on the Housetop." However, he would receive little in royalties from their publication—he purportedly received just six free copies of the sheet music for "Nelly Gray"—and died of tuberculosis at the age of thirty-three. Nevertheless, Benjamin Hanby's contribution to the history of the Underground Railroad should stand.

LITTLE IS KNOWN OF Joseph Sanford before he became a fugitive sometime in the 1840s or early 1850s. He lived on a plantation in Kentucky, where his master was a man named J. Graves. He may have been a relative of Bartlett Graves, an early Kentucky landowner whose 550-acre plantation, Walnut Grove, in Kenton County is now the site of the city of Erlanger.

Sanford related that his master was a "most cruel man" who would regularly entrust him to go to Cincinnati to do the marketing. Because he took great pride in his position as the foreman on the plantation, Sanford was reluctant to try to escape because he did not want to be carried back in disgrace if he failed. But then his master hired an overseer who whipped him for going to church. Sanford had not been whipped for twenty years and he felt humiliated by it.

The following spring, about the first of May, the overseer was away when Sanford got into a dispute with Graves about weeding, plowing and replanting the fields. The master did not feel the slaves were working fast enough and decided to take away their holidays. This was the last straw. Sanford and a dozen other slaves—not all from the same place—decided to "break and run away, hit or miss, live or die." As Sanford recalled years later,

On a Sunday night we made our break, and when we got to Covington, it was daybreak; the garrison were up, beating their drums. God was on our side, or we should have been gone. We divided at the last toll-gate. Some going through the gate and myself and little Henry going round. We then found a skiff and oars, got in the skiff and crossed the Ohio into Cincinnati.[243]

When he realized his slaves were missing, Graves naturally suspected they were headed for Ohio, which was only ten miles away. He hurried there with a party of men, hoping to overtake them. On reaching Cincinnati,

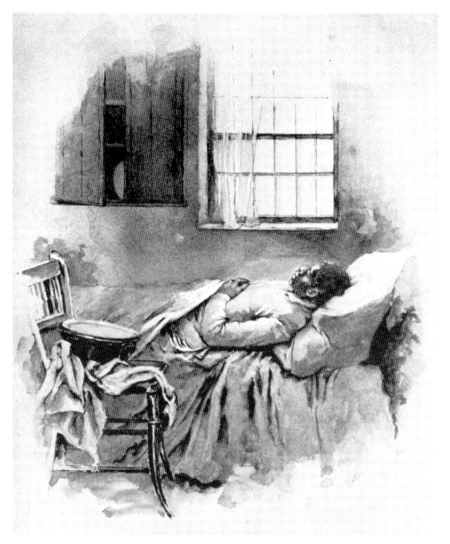

Escaping to Ohio, Joe Selby told his story before he died to some abolitionists who took him in. *Authors' collection.*

Graves and his men were informed that some runaways had recently passed through the city, but their route was unknown. Therefore, Graves offered a large reward for their apprehension and returned to his plantation.

Sanford and his family had ventured into Cincinnati, walking up Main Street until they encountered a group of slave hunters who questioned them quite thoroughly. Pretending to befriend them, one of the men placed them in a cellar for safekeeping while investigating the possibility of a reward.

John Hatfield was working as a barber on a steamboat that plied a regular route between New Orleans and Cincinnati. A free "mulatto" born in Pennsylvania, he was an acknowledged leader among the "colored people of the city," advocating for the repeal of the Black Laws.[244] When he heard about the fugitives, he and some companions went to investigate. They found a man plugging up all the holes in the cellar to prevent the curious from looking in at the captives. Hatfield managed to ask Mrs. Sanford if she knew the man who was "helping" them. She replied that she had never seen him before. Hatfield then told her, "You must get out of this."[245]

Assigning one of his friends to keep an eye on the guard, Hatfield and his accomplices took the fugitives out of the cellar two at a time and hid them throughout the city. When their pursuers discovered their prisoners were missing, they offered a reward to anyone who would tell them where they were. "But the rewards would not fetch them: a million of dollars would not take a slave in Cincinnati out of some people's hands."[246]

Afterward, Hatfield returned home, but near dark, a friend showed up and said that the slave catchers had come to his residence in search of the woman he was hiding (apparently not Mrs. Sanford but possibly a daughter). As the men were occupied at the back door, Hatfield wrapped her in a blanket, took her out a front window and stashed her at a friend's house across the street. When someone asked him what he was doing, he told them he was tending to a sick man. Soon, however, that house was surrounded as well. So Hatfield and the others dressed the woman in a young man's clothes. Then,

> We came out at a gate nearby, we crossed over the street; —there were five or six persons then coming towards us—all I could say was, "walk heavy!" for they came right upon us. They walked with us half a square—I was scared only for her. They stopped a little—we got fifty yards ahead of them. I then told her, "they are coming again,—hold your head up, and walk straight and heavy!" By this time they were up with us again: they walked with us a whole square, looking right in her face, trying to recognize her. We came to where there was a light opposite,—I did not want to have her come to the light,—I turned the corner and said, "Come this way, Jim." She understood, and followed me. Upon this, they turned and walked away as fast as they could walk.[247]

Hatfield left the woman he nicknamed "Jim" in a safe place and then returned to where he had left the slave hunters, thinking he would have some fun with them. He found about a dozen of them standing on the corner near the house that was under surveillance, discussing the situation. They claimed "they had seen the 'nigger' dressed in men's clothes, but that they were afraid to take her, there were so many 'niggers' around."[248] But Hatfield insisted he was alone with her, and the men did not want to admit they had been intimidated by him.

The Sanfords remained in hiding for a fortnight before Hatfield and his friends "guided them on the way to Michigan, which they reached in safety."[249] Although they were then recaptured, a judge subsequently ruled in their favor, and they were permitted to continue to Canada. Eventually, the fugitives reached the town of Amherstburg, Canada, where they settled down to enjoy their lives as free Blacks.

Nevertheless, Joseph Sanford lived in fear that he might be carried back to slavery at any time. In fact, the old man was "rather superstitious, and often [said] he [believed] that the slaveholders [had] some sort of charms by which they can make a slave follow them, if they can once get near enough for the charms to operate."[250] When he heard that Graves, his old master, had come to town, he would not even return to his own house for fear he might encounter Graves, insisting he was a "conjurer."

Joe Selby supposedly died in the house of Dr. Simon Hyde (*pictured*) in Rushville. *Courtesy of Zohoe/Wikipedia.*

John Hatfield later moved to Canada as well. He claimed that he had harbored as many as fifteen runaways in his house at one time and as many as twenty-seven in a year. Meanwhile, at the age of sixty-five, Sanford still suffered from his years of slavery, never having learned to read or write.

Having settled in Washington Courthouse, Ohio, the Reverend William M. Mitchell began working with a runaway slave named John Mason. Mason was an extraordinary individual who purportedly fled from slavery in the 1830s and made his way to Ohio when he was about twelve years old. He then went to work as a waiter, paying his way through Oberlin College, from which he graduated in the 1840s before becoming a conductor on the Underground Railroad.

In the course of nineteen months, Mason brought 265 fugitives to Mitchell's house. From there, Mitchell forwarded them to Canada via the Underground Railroad. Mitchell believed that Mason had helped 1,300 people altogether before he was himself captured and sold. Mason was in the processing of returning to Ohio from Kentucky with four fugitives when they were overtaken.

Although Mason was ready to stand and fight, he found that his companions were unwilling to do so. Therefore, he surrendered to the slave hunters. "He was eventually sold and was taken to New Orleans," Mitchell wrote. "Yet in one year, 5 months, and 20 days," Mason sent him a letter from Hamilton, Canada, where he had taken up residence after once again escaping from his master.[251] Meanwhile, in 1860, Mitchell published *The Under-Ground Railroad*, the first book to address the subject while aiding fugitive slaves was still illegal. By then, he was a minister in Toronto, Canada.

About September 20, 1856, a slave named Lewis, his wife and their six children left their home in Rowan County, Kentucky, near Maysville, and made their way to Ohio. According to Squire B. Million, the owner of the fugitives, they were taken in by David Wait (or Watt or Waits) of Adams County, who unlawfully concealed them and also aided and abetted their escape to Canada.

The case was heard by Judge Leavitt of the U.S. District Court in Cincinnati on November 10, 1857. In Wait's defense, Attorney John Jolliffe introduced testimony claiming that Million voluntarily sent Lewis and his family to a Free State so they would be beyond the reach of a creditor to whom he owed a substantial debt. Wait provided them with shelter only to the extent he would have any other traveler and had no involvement in their subsequent flight to Canada.

During the trial, Million, "the principal witness against Wait, gave testimony so contradictory to what he had avowed to several persons previously, that he was immediately put on trial for perjury."[252] According to the *Cincinnati Gazette*, credible witnesses testified that Million said Lewis and the other slaves crossed the Ohio River with his consent. In his charge to the jury, Judge Leavitt stated "that, if the slaves left Kentucky by consent of their master, the verdict should be in their [the slaves'] favor."[253] However, the jury was deadlocked after a day (nine votes for conviction, three for acquittal), so the judge discharged them and released Million.

Although Jolliffe asked for an immediate retrial, Judge Leavitt declined, holding the case over to the next term. The following day, Squire Million swore an oath before U.S. Commissioner George M. Lee. He charged that James J. Putney, a witness in Wait's trial, "did about the 20th of September, 1856, harbor and conceal eight fugitives from labor, so as to prevent their delivery and arrest by their claimant and master, to whom they owned service."[254] The warrant was handed to U.S. Deputy Marshal Churchill, who promptly arrested Putney.

Prior to this, however, a William Shaw, the principal witness for the defense, swore out his own warrant against Million, charging him with committing perjury. Shaw claimed that "Mr. Million admitted, while the Jury were out, that the negro Lewis told him that he should leave Kentucky the night he did, and that there was an agreement that the negro should return, or the master should come after him, as soon as some pecuniary troubles were ended."[255]

As a result, Million was also arrested by Churchill and taken before Commissioner Lee. With Jolliffe representing Putney and Judge Spooner Million, Lee conducted an examination of the charge. When he finished, he discharged Million. The Putney case was postponed until November 18, with both the defendant and the plaintiff required to post $500 bonds. In the end, Putney was acquitted when a Miss Wait, David Wait's niece, testified that she did not see the accused at her uncle's house on the night the slaves departed.

Slave trading was such a lucrative enterprise that slave hunters often invested considerable time and money in tracking down, capturing and transporting their quarry. St. Louis newspapers reported that two men calling themselves

Simpkins and Orr were arrested on the evening of Saturday, June 8, 1856, by officers St. Ange and Marley, who took them to jail. The men had two African American youth in their custody named Ralls and Logan. As the boys related, Orr saw them in Cincinnati, where they lived, and persuaded them to go with him to a farm about fifteen miles away on the river. Taking passage on a boat, they traveled down to Cairo, Illinois, where they then took a train to St. Louis.

On their arrival, Orr attempted to sell them to one or two slave traders, claiming that he was on his way to settle in Kansas. However, the traders did not trust him. After remaining in St. Louis a short while, Orr and the two boys then set off for St. Charles County, crossing the river at Music's ferry. Orr then hired one of the ferrymen, a man named Simpkins, to go with them to Kansas. When they reached Portage, Orr tried to sell the two youth again but failed. They eventually returned to St. Louis.

The *Cincinnati Gazette* reported that Orr's suspicious activities finally came to the attention of the police, who began hunting for him and his companions. When the party was apprehended, the boys at first protested that they actually belonged to Orr before admitting the truth.

After the story came out, Governor Salmon P. Chase sent a requisition to the governor of Missouri for the return of Orr to Ohio. The municipal authorities of Cincinnati even raised a small amount of money to finance the delivery of the requisition by a messenger named Anderson. However, when Anderson arrived in St. Louis, he learned that Orr had been released on a writ of habeas corpus and was nowhere to be found.

"The two colored boys are yet in prison," newspapers reported, "and a person from Kentucky, is said to be on his way to St. Louis, to claim one of them as his slave."[256] After returning to Cincinnati for further instructions, Anderson quickly telegraphed the mayor of St. Louis to detain the youth until he could return with papers that proved they were free.

Chapter 12

TUNNELS AND SECRET ROOMS

An architectural preservationist once said, "All old houses need a story." And a good story can literally be an old house's salvation. Otherwise, most inevitably bow to the wrecking ball, even those that are architecturally distinguished. No wonder preservationists are constantly scrambling for old house stories, regardless of how suspect they may be.

In Ohio, any house of a certain age is liable to hailed as an Underground Railroad house, often based solely on "oral tradition"—that is, hearsay.[257] Frequently, an "old-timer" will recall exploring a hidden room or secret tunnel as a child. Many such recollections seem to be "recovered memories" of the "I hadn't thought of it in years" variety, spurred by the discovery of some architectural anomaly or what passes for one to the untrained eye. And the fact that an abolitionist once lived there isn't proof that any UGRR activity took place on the premises.

UGRR authority Wilbur Siebert noted that there was a "tradition" of a tunnel under the river at the Major Bartholomew house eleven miles south of Delaware in southern Liberty Township. But a statement Siebert obtained from a later owner of the house suggested an alternative explanation: "Just north of the house is an eighteen-foot ravine. The fugitive slaves came up the Olentangy [River], then up the ravine to the Bartholomew house, entered the side door near the back of the house and were kept in the kitchen."[258]

The Bartholomew house still exists. Donna Meyer, executive director of the Delaware County Historical Society, has said that "while no hidden passages have been discovered inside the house, its basement and attic easily could have served as hiding places."[259] But—and this is the crucial point—

there is no record that they did. Alas, contemporary documentation of UGRR activity is rare.

Johnny Jones, a columnist for the *Columbus Dispatch*, wrote an article in 1954 about the former residence of Judge George M. Parsons. Jones visited the magnificent old dwelling as it was being demolished and learned that "under the gigantic limestone steps was a very thick walled room under the front approach or doorway. When the wreckers investigated they had to break through a solid doorway. Two iron grills gave air and light. It would have been an ideal spot to hide slaves."[260]

Although Judge Parsons was a Republican and an ardent supporter of Abraham Lincoln, his participation in the UGRR was wishful thinking on Jones's part. And there was nothing particularly special about the room discovered under the porch.

Abolitionist John Rankin's home still sits atop a three-hundred-foot bluff overlooking Ripley. In 1925, an unidentified reporter wrote, "The cabin was a mass of trap doors and secret passages, where the unfortunate blacks could secrete themselves for the night and escape via an underground tunnel, which led for some distance down the hill."[261] However, there is not a scrap of evidence supporting this claim.

Eli Coffin welcomes freedom seekers into his home. *Authors' collection.*

"After passage of the Fugitive Slave Act of 1850, which made any interference with the capture and return of fugitive slaves a serious Federal crime, Colonel Samuel Moore of Circleville became active in the Underground Railroad"—or so it says on the historical marker erected next to the Samuel Moore House in Circleville. But is it true?

A 1947 article referenced by Siebert mentioned the discovery of a hole in the cellar of the Circleville home of William Asbury Moore at the corner of Court and Mound Streets. According to reporter Paul Quick, "The hole, about two feet square, widened sharply back of the stone facings and a few feet underground, it turned and opened into a full-sized tunnel."[262] Quick quoted the current occupant of the house, Lillian Moore, widow of Howard Moore, who remembered "that it went under Circleville all the way to the town limit"—a distance of half a mile from the center of town.[263]

Mrs. Moore's son had happened on the tunnel beneath a marble slab in the floor. When he ventured into it, he stopped after going about fifteen feet due to "debris and fear of gases." Another lifelong resident of Circleville, Lawrence Goeller, told the reporter, "We used to play in it as kids, 45 years ago. We never knew it ended at the Moore home."[264] He was talking about another hole in the ground that passed behind a dairy on the edge of town.

However, a 1947 article in the *Circleville Herald* reported, "City Councilman William M. Reid, who prides himself on being a Circleville and Pickaway county historian, declared flatly that the idea of the Moore home having long ago been a 'station' on the slave underground railway is 'pure bosh.'"[265]

Reid, who had just turned seventy-nine, said there was once a swamp known as Lake Darling in the area of the Moore home many years before. A large tunnel was constructed to serve as a drainage sewer for the swamp. He claimed from personal knowledge—having once been Moore's neighbor—that the aperture in the basement of the Moore home was really a "coal dump."[266]

Furthermore, Lillian Moore, widow of Howard Moore, said her husband's forefathers came to Ohio from the Southern states. She had no knowledge of Colonel Samuel Ashbury Moore or any of the others having been an "ardent abolitionist."[267]

Nevertheless, a number of writers have claimed that the home is haunted by the spirit of a slave who died there and that others who passed away after leaving Moore's care have returned to seek shelter. The fact that there is no substance to these stories, many of which seem to be of fairly recent origin, hasn't deterred ghost hunters in the least.

The Spread Eagle Tavern in Hanoverton had a tunnel that was allegedly used by the UGRR. *Authors' collection.*

In 1949, Leslie Zimmerman of Samantha discovered "an opening in the inside wall of a well" at a farm he had recently purchased. It led to "an underground chamber that once might have been used as a hiding place for fugitive slaves."[268] In order to access it, Zimmerman had to lower himself seven feet below the surface of the well and squeeze through a twenty-inch square opening. It led to a nine-foot-by-nine-foot room with a seven-foot ceiling. However, there was no known connection between the farm and the UGRR. Significantly, "a small brick building used for milk storage" was directly above the room, suggesting that the stone chamber, a type of cistern, might have helped keep the milk cool.[269]

Historians Bryon Fruehling and Robert Smith set out to examine some of these tales of secret hiding places from an architectural and archaeological perspective.[270] Unable to investigate them all or even a random sampling, they selected an area in northeastern Ohio—Ashland, Wayne and Holmes Counties—and inspected more than a dozen purported UGRR houses that were said to contain one of these features.

In short, they found that all the secret chambers or "dungeons" turned out to be cisterns or unexcavated crawlspaces and that there was no sign of tunnels. Furthermore, several of the houses weren't even built until after the Civil War. The investigators noted that few accounts by fugitives themselves or agents of the UGRR mention such things. Rather, runaway slaves were harbored in homes, barns and outbuildings or in nearby fields or woods. Of course, that doesn't prove that someone, somewhere didn't once construct a secret room or tunnel for UGRR purposes, but it doesn't prove they did, either.

OFTEN, THE FEAR OF being sold Down South prompted enslaved people to make a dash for freedom when they otherwise might have been content to remain where they were. The Monroes were a large family of slaves living in Boone County, Kentucky: a mother, Georgiana; ten daughters; and one son. The girls ranged from six to nineteen years old, while the boy was described as a young man.

When the mother learned they were to be sold far to the south, she resolved to do something about it. But she had little advance warning because her master decided it would be best to keep the matter as quiet as possible. So she asked her son about the advisability of escaping to Ohio. He readily agreed that would be the best course of action, although both knew it would be an arduous undertaking.

In October 1856, the Monroe family set out on their perilous journey to freedom. They lived but forty miles from the Ohio River, so their plan was to go there as directly as possible. Waiting until late at night, they each took a small bundle of clothing and set out. At daybreak, they found they had traveled about twelve miles and were now in the midst of a dense forest. They remained there until nightfall and then continued on.

Although the son was familiar with the route, the fugitives frequently had to take cover in the forest to avoid encountering others along the way. By the third night, they had reached the southern bank of the Ohio River. Finding a small boat, they made the crossing without incident. Once on the opposite bank, however, they did not know which way to turn.

Unknowingly, they were in the vicinity of New Richmond, Ohio. About a mile distant, the son left his mother and sisters in the forest and set off to town to try to make contact with some friends. He succeeded in locating H.J., "a good and tried friend," and several others, according to historian Benjamin Drew, who immediately sketched out plans for aiding the family's flight northward.[271]

That night, friends of the young man visited the Monroes in the forest. By now, they knew that their owner was searching for them and had offered a reward of $2,000 for their capture. Considerable excitement had gripped

Conneaut's David Cummins Octagon House was rumored to have a tunnel that ran to Conneaut Creek. *Courtesy of Ymblanter/Wikipedia.*

the community, and the slave hunters were out in force. The son's friends kept their eyes peeled for any signs of them while the slaves were bundled into a covered wagon with bags of straw and transported to another UGRR station. They continued to be conveyed from one station to another until they reached the small town of Ann Arbor, Michigan.

Anticipating their movements, their master had arrived there ahead of them. He hoped to cut them off in Detroit, where they were expected to cross the river in Canada. But the fugitives learned they were being closely pursued and took the advice of their friends to take the train directly to Detroit. In two and a half hours, they stood on the shore of the Detroit River.

Once he realized they had given him the slip, the slaveholder took the next train from Ann Arbor to Detroit. Meanwhile, the Monroe family boarded a steamboat, the *Argo*, which would take them to the Canadian shore in fifteen minutes or less. Racing full speed down Jefferson Avenue, the master called out for the captain to stop, but he laughed and continued until he had landed the woman and her eleven children on Canadian soil.

Reverend William Troy wrote,

> *It was my fortune to meet her soon after she walked off the boat. I asked her several questions in relation to her situation. She said she had no friends except her children, and was deeply affected when she mentioned how narrowly she escaped. Her tears rolled down her cheeks, and literally fell upon the ground. I truly felt for her. The tears of the poor can always work into my heart.*[272]

Troy arranged for housing, food and clothing. The older daughters were provided with jobs as domestics, while the younger ones were enrolled in school. In a letter to her father, Troy's daughter informed him that Georgiana Monroe passed away in 1860, four years after leading her family to freedom.

In May 1857, a band of Kentucky residents and a few U.S. deputy marshals decided to go slave hunting in Champaign County. But their efforts were frustrated by some local residents. Returning to Cincinnati, they obtained warrants for the arrest of four Ohio citizens they accused of undermining their endeavor. They succeeded in arresting several of them. However, the citizens' friends promptly procured writs of habeas corpus, which they handed off to the Champaign County sheriff.

Unwilling to allow themselves to be apprehended, the slave hunters roughed the sheriff up and fired a few pistol shots at him while beating a retreat. So the friends obtained another writ and placed it in the hands of the Greene County sheriff. After pulling together a posse, the Greene County sheriff set off after the slave hunters. Although one of the deputy marshals fired at them, the sheriff and his men were able to subdue the party and carted them off to Xenia, the county seat. While the deputies posted bail, the others were lodged in jail to await trial.

"Judge Leavitt, at Cincinnati," one historian wrote, "then issued a writ of *habeas corpus*, directed to the sheriff, requiring him to produce his prisoners."[273] This was the same judge who remanded Margaret Garner and her family back to slavery.[274]

Governor Salmon Chase dispatched his attorney general to argue the case on behalf of the state. Mr. Pugh and Clement Vallandigham represented

Quaker Moses McKay's house in Corwin was built with the help of twenty freed slaves and was purportedly a stop on the UGRR. *Courtesy of Library of Congress.*

the slave hunters. Nevertheless, Judge Leavitt ordered the prisoners released. "The decision of Judge Leavitt in this case, like that in the Garner case, denied the right of the State to execute its own criminal process, or civil process, where that execution interfered with the claims of masters under the Fugitive-slave Act."[275]

MANY BLACK MEN WERE lured into captivity by the offer of a job. Although they understood the risks involved in accompanying a stranger, they found it difficult to refuse. But sometimes the hunter got caught in his own snare.

Two young African American men, ages eighteen or twenty, were arrested in Cleveland on November 16, 1857. They were said to have escaped from their owner, a man named Jewett, in Tennessee, and had been working in a local hotel for some time. After the court remanded them to their master, they were placed on a train to Cincinnati. From there, they were to be shipped by river to their former home.

When they reached Carlisle Station, one of the slaves got off the train and refused to get back on. Jewett "endeavored to force him upon the platform, but the fugitive turned upon him, struck one or two telling blows, and then made good speed for the country."[276] Since it was impossible to stop the train to apprehend him, Jewett had no choice but to continue on to Middletown with the other slave. Once there, he obtained assistance and returned to Carlisle to resume the chase. Meanwhile, the second fugitive was brought to Cincinnati to stand for a hearing.

However, the Dayton *Journal*'s account was somewhat at odds with the initial report. It stated that the Black man who left the train at Carlisle had not fled but remained at the station. Furthermore, he insisted that "he was not a slave, but that he and the other boy had been hired by the white man Jewett to go to a Columbus hotel."[277] When they reached Carlisle, they discovered that Jewett had "taken the Delaware Route, and was hurrying them towards slavery, through its entrance gate—Cincinnati."[278]

After the Black man refused to reboard the train, Jewett continued on to Middletown and then returned to Carlisle with a companion. They found the purported fugitive at the Carlisle Station depot and engaged in an argument. As a result, all three men were evicted from the building. Jewett then hired a wagon, and the three men set off for Franklin. Along the way, Jewett tried to persuade the wagon driver to continue on to Cincinnati for sixty dollars. Instead, when they reached Franklin, the driver told the authorities of the bribe attempt, and all three men were arrested.

On being questioned separately, one of the White men said the Black man was a fugitive from Tennessee, the other that he had escaped from Kentucky. The magistrate had them all conveyed to the jail in Lebanon for further investigation since Jewett did not have a writ or other papers to show proof of ownership. While on the way to the jail, Jewett offered the police officer one hundred dollars to permit him to escape. The fate of the other Black man who had been taken to Cincinnati earlier was unknown.

Chapter 13

DOUBLE-CODED SPIRITUALS

frican American spirituals such as "Steal Away to Jesus," "Swing Low, Sweet Chariot," "Wade in the Water," "Gospel Train" and many others have come to be associated with the Underground Railroad. It is said that some contain hidden messages that encouraged and aided slaves in their escape to freedom. But do they?

It is easy to identify many of the biblical texts from which the spirituals are drawn, right down to specific phrases. For example, "God's gonna trouble the water" from "Wade in the Water" is taken from John 5:2–9: "For an angel went down at a certain season into the pool, and troubled the water."

However, it is not unreasonable to think that for many people of color, especially those being held in captivity, the spirituals had a double meaning or "double-coding." This allegorical duality was facilitated by their identification with the Israelites, who, the Bible said, had also been enslaved. So the River Jordan became the Ohio River and Canaan Land became Canada, Ohio or even Michigan.

Although the origins of most spirituals are lost to history, "Steal Away" and "Swing Low" are said to have been composed by Wallace Willis sometime prior to 1862. A slave, Wallace originally lived on a plantation in Holly Springs, Mississippi, owned by Brit Willis, a half-Choctaw Indian. When the U.S. government forced the Choctaw tribe to relocate to southern Oklahoma in the 1830s, Wallace and his wife, Minerva, were relocated as well. Settling near Doaksville, Oklahoma, Wallace was hired out by his owner to perform work at Spencer Academy, a Choctaw boys' school. Then,

Work songs were sometimes sung while picking cotton. *Authors' collection.*

in 1849, Alexander Reid, a minister from New England, was hired as the school's superintendent. Over the course of a dozen years, he often heard "Uncle" Wallace, as the slave was called, perform the songs for the students.

After the Civil War broke out in 1861, Wallace; his wife, Minerva; and several of their children were taken to Old Boggy Depot for protection, and Reid never saw them again. When his own wife died later that year, Reid returned home to Princeton, New Jersey.

Ten years later, in December 1871, Reid attended a concert by the Fisk Jubilee Singers in Newark, New Jersey. Following the performance, Professor George L. White, leader of the ensemble, announced that they would be repeating the same songs in subsequent appearances because they lacked additional material. Remembering the songs Wallace used to sing, Reid contacted White. The choir leader "was delighted to hear of the existence of more 'plantation songs' and was willing to have them taught to the Jubilees."[279]

Because Reid could not read music, he wrote down the lyrics and then sang the songs over and over again to the choir until they memorized them. In particular, he taught them six songs, including "Swing Low, Sweet Chariot" and "Steal Away to Jesus."[280] When they played New York City later that same month, "Swing Low" was already part of their repertoire.

Fisk University in Nashville, Tennessee, is a historically Black college that opened its doors in 1866. George White, a White man who served as the school treasurer, was called on to provide the students with musical instruction. Selecting those students he felt had potential, White taught them the standard classical repertoire but also allowed them to sing their "own music."[281]

Following a well-received concert in 1867, White began to take the group out on trips to nearby communities. Four years later, he decided they should go on the road in order to raise money for the building program at Fisk. Financed by borrowed funds, White left on October 6, 1871, with a pianist, eleven vocalists and a female teacher-chaperone.

When they played Cincinnati, the local press was critical, referring to them as "Beecher's Negro Minstrels" because celebrated preacher Henry Ward Beecher, Harriett Beecher Stowe's brother, had sponsored them. Moving

The Fisk Jubilee Singers popularized Black spirituals. *Courtesy of Library of Congress.*

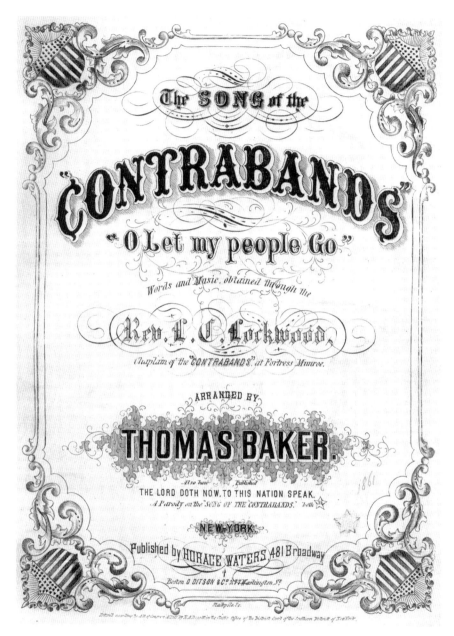

"Go Down Moses" was first published in 1862 as "The Song of the Contrabands," after Reverend Lewis Lockwood heard "contrabands" singing it at Fort Monroe. *Courtesy of Library of Congress.*

on to Columbus, White spent a sleepless night. While lying awake, however, he recalled that slaves had often talked about the "year of jubilee," and he hit on the idea of giving his group a new name: Fisk Jubilee Singers.[282] The name caught on with the public. So Columbus was the birthplace of the renamed Fisk Jubilee Singers.

In his history of the Fisk Jubilee Singers, Andrew Ward credits the group's pianist, Ella Sheppard Moore, with bringing many of the songs to the group, including "'Swing Low, Sweet Chariot,' and 'Before I'd Be a Slave'—songs her enslaved mother, Sarah, had taught her and later claimed to have composed."[283] Ella was born on a Tennessee planation in 1851. Later, her mother was sold Down South to Mississippi. As recorded in Ella's diary, the group added a "new 'Swing Low'" to their repertoire in March 1875, suggesting other versions were in circulation.

Over the years, these spirituals have taken on added significance through their purported connection with UGRR activity. "Steal Away" in particular has become associated with Harriett Tubman, who purportedly used to sing it to herald her arrival or signal that the time was right to flee. According to Tubman biographer Kate Clifford Larson in *Bound for the Promised Land*, "If danger lurked nearby, Tubman would sing an appropriate spiritual to warn her party of an impending threat to their safety."[284] But this is inconsistent with "Steal Away" having been written by a slave in far-off Oklahoma.

DANIEL PRUE AND JOHN F. Hite were targets of a phony job scheme. Prue, son of a fugitive slave, and Hite (or Hight), an emancipated slave, were living in Geneva, New York, when they were offered positions at a hotel in Columbus, Ohio, by a man named Napoleon Bonaparte Van Tuyl. Age twenty-one or so, Van Tuyl was a clerk in a dry goods store but was said to come from a respectable family; he was their "only remaining child," according to the *Yates County Chronicle*. The young man was also "a professor of religion and a member of a religious church."[285]

Early in December 1857, while Prue, Hite and Van Tuyl were traveling by train from Cleveland to Columbus, Van Tuyl chanced to meet three Kentuckians: Barton W. Jenkins of Henry County and Henry Giltner and George W. Metcalf of Carroll County. Identifying himself as Paul Lensington, Van Tuyl told the strangers that his traveling companions were fugitive slaves. He then asked the Kentuckians to assist him in returning the slaves to Tennessee, where they were ostensibly from.

Prue, however, overheard their conversation. Realizing that the train had already passed through Columbus, he made an attempt to get off when it stopped near Dayton at Carlisle. Jenkins tried to intervene, but Prue knocked him down, jumped from the car and headed back to Columbus on foot. Along with Van Tuyl, Jenkins returned to Columbus to search for Prue, only to be arrested in Franklin County on a charge of kidnapping. However, the charge against Jenkins was later dismissed for want of evidence.

Unaware of what had befallen Prue, Hite remained on board the train with the other two strangers. He continued to believe "that the men were acting in good faith, and that everything would be satisfactory."[286] He rode on to Cincinnati and then was taken across the Ohio River to Covington. From there, he was shipped down the river to Carrolton, Kentucky, and jailed as a runaway slave.

Van Tuyl arrived in Kentucky a day or two later and sold Hite to Jenkins for $500 using his Lensington alias. The bill of sale stated that he was "19 years of age, of copper color, that he was the true and lawful owner of said boy, and that he was a slave for life."[287] The original price was to be $750, but Van Tuyl subtracted $250 for the trouble Jenkins had gone to in helping him secure his "property."

Jenkins then turned around and sold Hite to Lorenzo Graves for $750. Graves initially took Hite to Warsaw, Kentucky, but later sent him to Louisville, where he was locked up until such time as his services were needed. In spite of his perilous situation, Hite had not been forgotten by his friends back in New York. As the *Cincinnati Gazette* reported, Judge Phineas B. Wilcox in Columbus received certified copies of Hite's freedom papers, as well as a letter from the Honorable Samuel F. Vinton providing a detailed description of the young man.

Apparently, Hite had been a servant to the Vinton family in Washington. These documents were entrusted to Judge Calvin Walker, who was dispatched to Kentucky by John A. King, the governor of New York, along with Robert Lay of Geneva, for whom Hite had also worked. Walker was instructed to get to the bottom of the matter.

Having tailed Hite to Warsaw, Walker and Lay were able to locate Graves with little difficulty. On being shown the documents, Graves replied, "I am satisfied he is a free negro, and that he has been kidnapped. I am a Kentuckian and a slaveholder, but I would as soon poison my mother as to purchase a negro I knew to be free."[288] He promised he would turn Hite over to Walker and Lay so he could be taken to a Free State.

"Get Off the Track!" published in 1844, linked emancipation with a physical railroad. *Courtesy the Lester S. Levy Sheet Music Collection.*

Naturally, Graves first sought out Jenkins, who professed to be as astonished as Graves was by Van Tuyl's trickery. He immediately gave back the money Graves had paid him, asking only that Walker and Lay reimburse him should they recover any money from "Mr. Lensington." The entire party then set off for Louisville, where Hite was still locked up. On gaining the young man's release, Graves accompanied Walker, Lay and Hite to Cincinnati, where he gave Hite money to spend on his trip home and purchased several presents for the young man's mother.

Early on December 15, 1857, Hite arrived in Geneva by train in the company of Walker and Lay. He was ecstatic over regaining his freedom, having feared he would be sold further south. Meanwhile, Van Tuyl had gone to Dayton, where he mailed a letter to a lady friend in Geneva in which he revealed his travel plans. Somehow, it was intercepted. When he arrived in Niagara Falls, New York, in December, he was immediately arrested at the suspension bridge spanning the Niagara River and transported back to Geneva.

A slightly different story has it that Van Tuyl was masquerading as a free-spending Southern gentleman named H.B. Livingston when he arrived at Niagara Falls. "While there he purchased a lot of Indian work, which he forwarded by express to a Miss Leman, of Geneva, to whom he was engaged to be married, but the package was intercepted, and an officer from Geneva went up and made the arrest."[289]

Van Tuyl likely did not anticipate the reception he received. "He was met at the Geneva railroad station," said the *Albany Journal*, "by an immense crowd of intensely excited and indignant citizens, most of whom were black, and, but for the presence of a number of officers, would probably have been subjected to harsh treatment."[290]

One young African American woman attempted to strike him on the head with an iron bar but shattered a nearby lantern instead. Finally, the prisoner was whisked away in a hack and "lodged in a place of safety."[291] He subsequently paid his bail of $1,500 and disappeared, presumably into Canada. However, in April 1858, Van Tuyl was spotted by Jenkins in New Orleans. He was now going by the name of Edwin Read. Seizing the young man by the collar, Jenkins handed him over to the police. He was arrested and taken to Frankfort, Kentucky, where he was tried on a charge of obtaining money by false pretenses. Van Tuyl did not deny kidnapping Hite but claimed he was induced to do so by a couple of men he refused to identify.

"Public sympathy in Kentucky was very much in favor of Van Tuyl, probably on account of his youth, he not yet being 21 years of age."[292]

"I Would I Were a Slave Again," published in 1861, purports to be the lament of a former slave who longs for the good old days. *Courtesy the Lester S. Levy Sheet Music Collection.*

His parents were both present in the courtroom when the Kentucky jury acquitted him. He was then handed over to officers from New York to be tried for kidnapping in that state. Daniel Prue, who was working in a livery stable in Columbus, was summoned to New York as a witness against the accused. Local citizens raised enough money to enable him to return.

Despite twice skipping bail, faking his own death and a hung jury, Van Tuyl was eventually convicted and sentenced to two years' hard labor in the Auburn State Penitentiary for "inveigling." The courtroom was jammed with spectators, particularly women. He could have received as many as ten years, and it was a wonder he wasn't given the trouble he had caused enforcement.

No doubt runaways found the whole legal process quite intimidating. With their fate hanging in the balance, they did not always know which of the White men to trust—their master and his agents or the strangers who were allegedly representing their interests. As a result, they sometimes answered yes when they should have said no.

Three slaves belonging to Thornton Withers were in transit from St. Louis to his home in Fauquier County, Virginia, aboard the steamer *Melnotte*: a thirty-five-year-old man and two girls, age ten and twelve. On October 3, 1857, they stopped at a boat landing in Cincinnati.

While they were still standing on the wharf, a free Black man rushed to obtain a writ of habeas corpus from Judge John Burgoyne of Probate Court, and they were seized by the authorities. When the slaves were brought before the judge on Monday afternoon, he continued their case at the request of Withers. In the meantime, they were placed in the custody of Darius Eggleston, who took them to his home on Ninth Street.

Withers subsequently obtained a writ of habeas corpus from Judge Alfred G.W. Carter of the court of common pleas, charging that the three slaves were being illegally restrained of their liberty. Carter had previously presided over the tragic Margaret Garner case. Asserting that the slaves owed him service, Winters asked for their return. In compliance with the writ, Sheriff Glass conveyed the slaves to the court of Judge Carter.

As hundreds of people awaited the hearing of the writ before Judge Burgoyne, Judge Carter conducted his own. He asked each one of the slaves the following questions, and they were said to respond in like fashion:

Are you a slave?
I am.
Are you restrained of your liberty?
I am not.
Do you wish to go with your master?
I do.[293]

A man named M.D. Conway wrote to the *Anti-Slavery Bugle* that he spoke with the slaves while they were in the custody of Eggleston. He learned that the man preferred to return to Withers because he had a wife and five children in the family of Jordon Saunders of Warrenton. The two girls, on the other hand, were nine- and eleven-year-old orphans and had no ties to Virginia. Neither did they have any particular preference for what was to become of them, although at one point they said they didn't want to leave Mrs. Eggleston. It was evident that they had no appreciation for their situation and were treating it as a joke.

After being told they were free to go where they chose (or "do as they please," as Conway put it) Judge Carter then directed the sheriff to turn the slaves over to their master. Immediately ushered out of the courtroom, they were placed in a waiting express wagon, driven down Vine Street and put on board the ferry boat *Queen City.* A few minutes later, they were in Newport, Kentucky. The three slaves "went on their way rejoicing to 'Old Virginia'"—or so the newspapers reported.[294]

According to Conway, they "returned to the most corrupt hole of a village to be found in Northern Virginia, a place where it is known that not one colored woman in a hundred ever reaches maternity undefiled."[295] Withers purportedly did not deny this when Conway asked him about it.

"And here, into a coarse low tavern on the suburbs of this profligate place, among coarse and utterly ignorant people, a Cincinnati Judge who has turned two intelligent and likely little girls, to be irretrievably lost!" the *Boston Liberator*

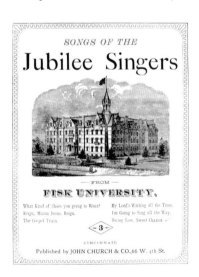

Songs of the Jubilee Singers was first published in 1884. *Courtesy of Library of Congress.*

reported.[296] Conway concluded by warning, "If this community does not require account of these immortal souls from his own hands, God will require it of theirs."[297]

When word of what had transpired reached Judge Burgoyne's courtroom, Attorney John Joliffe asked the court "to issue a writ against Alfred George Washington Carter, commanding him to show cause why he should not be punished for a contempt of this Court."[298] Understandably, Burgoyne was reluctant to take such action against a fellow judge.

The *Anti-Slavery Bugle* pointed out, "A statute of this State, passed April 17, 1857, expressly declares that persons brought to this State, by any other person, 'with intent to hold or control them as slaves, shall be deemed and held in all Courts as absolutely free.'"[299]

Donn Piatt said that "Judge Carter had informed him that he had issued the writ without a knowledge of all the facts, and that he should take no action in the matter until Judge Burgoyne got through," yet ten minutes later, he returned the trio to slavery.[300] It was also revealed that Carter had personally helped put the slaves in the vehicle that carried them off.

Chapter 14

FOUR MILLION STRONG

No one knows how many enslaved people actually escaped to freedom. Estimates generally range from twenty-five thousand to fifty thousand and the number was possibly as high as one hundred thousand (per the National Underground Railroad Freedom Center in Cincinnati). But it wasn't nearly as many as slaveholders feared or abolitionists claimed. In reality, most of those who attempted to run away were soon captured and returned to their owners. And due to the high birthrate among the enslaved, the total loss was more than offset by the natural population growth.

Rush Sloane, a prominent figure in Sandusky's Underground Railroad, later wrote, "It was said by the poet that 'distance lends enchantment to the view'; and in regard to the escape of fugitive slaves by the 'Underground Road,' I am convinced that the number passing over this line has been greatly magnified in the long period of time since this road ceased to run its always irregular trains."[301]

According to Henry Louis Gates Jr., in *100 Amazing Facts About the Negro*:

> *We can put these estimates in perspective by remembering that in 1860 there were 3.9 million slaves, and only 488,070 free Negroes (more than half of whom were still living in the South), while in 1850 there were 434,495 free Negroes. Since these figures would include those fugitives who had made it to the North on the Underground Railroad, plus natural increase, we can see how small the numbers of fugitive slaves who actually made it to the North in this decade, for example, unfortunately were.*[302]

The National Park Service suggests that from 1820 to 1860, "the most frequent calculation is that around one thousand per year actually escaped."[303] An article in the *Journal of Black Studies* essentially doubles that number.

But no one really knows. The problem is that few of those involved in the UGRR kept records, and Canadian census figures purportedly account for just six thousand of them. Furthermore, not all freedom seekers headed north. More than fifty thousand runaway slaves are thought to have remained in the southern states.

In Ohio, Levi Coffin and his wife are often credited with helping more than three thousand runaways gain their freedom. John Rankin and his family are said to have helped two thousand more. Rankin's neighbor John Parker is thought to have aided several hundred. And William Mitchell claimed nearly three hundred rescues. But since few UGRR conductors personally escorted fugitives from the Ohio River to Canada, there is a likelihood that some of the fugitives were double, triple or quadruple counted as they passed from hand to hand on their journey.

The border states—Kentucky, Virginia (including what is now West Virginia) and Maryland—contributed the most runaways to the UGRR. According to Professor Wilbur Siebert, Ohio had the most extensive UGRR network of any state. Siebert estimated there were three thousand miles of routes crisscrossing the state, with more than twenty points of entry on the Ohio River and at least ten points of exit along Lake Erie. However, the Ohio was a different river back then. As historian Dan Hurley has pointed out,

> *The river in the 19th century was not like the river today. Before the dams were built, the river was much shallower. In winter, it often froze solid, and in summer there were many more places where the river could be forded. A famous photograph of the river in the summer of 1883, in the middle channel, records the depth at one foot, eleven inches.*[304]

The river was also much narrower back then, perhaps a few hundred feet rather than several thousand. There are stories of Daniel Boone and other early frontiersmen crossing the Ohio River on horseback. And during dry periods, you supposedly wouldn't get your feet wet. While many runaway slaves chose to cross at such places as Cincinnati, Ripley, Portsmouth, Ironton, Pomeroy, Marietta and Gallipolis, they could also cross at many places in between, depending on the time of the year.

"The Proclamation of Emancipation," signed by President Abraham Lincoln and approved by his cabinet, applied only to slaves in the rebellious states. *Courtesy Wikipedia.*

Siebert found a single "leaf" from a diary kept by Daniel Osborn, a Quaker who lived in the Alum Creek Settlement, Delaware, Ohio. It recorded the number of African Americans who passed through the settlement during a five-month period in 1844: a total of forty-seven. From that, he extrapolated that between 1830 and 1860, "one may reckon that Ohio may have aided not less than 40,000 fugitives."[305] Or maybe not.

However, it is generally agreed that there were more freedom seekers following the passage of the highly controversial Fugitive Slave Act of 1850. The strengthening of the federal laws governing slavecatching had the reverse impact that the slave states had sought by polarizing the division between North and South. In fact, it appears that it "increased prices [for slaves] in border states by 15% to 30% more than in states further south," owing to greater numbers of runaways.[306]

Two slaves, ages twenty-two and twenty-five, "owned as brutes" by Robert Ingram (or Ingraham) of Dover, Mason County, Kentucky, escaped on March 5, 1858.[307] "Fine, muscular men, valued at $3000 in States where human beings are sold like mules," they managed to make their way to Canada, most likely by passing through Ohio.[308]

But they apparently could not enjoy their freedom, knowing that there were others they had left behind. So toward the end of August, the fugitives

Many of the formerly enslaved became refugees, having lost their homes. *Authors' collection.*

traveled to Cincinnati with a plan to help eight or ten other slaves with whom they had been corresponding to escape.

Unfortunately, they had placed too much trust in the sanctity of the U.S. mail: their letters were intercepted, and their plans were betrayed by a Black man who notified their master. Ingram subsequently came to Cincinnati and obtained a warrant for their arrest under the Fugitive Slave Law. He also engaged the services of Deputy Marshals B.P. Churchill and William L. Manson and Officers Harvey and Jeffreys. They suspected the men would arrive from Detroit on the Cincinnati, Hamilton & Dayton Railroad, and the depot was placed under surveillance for a day or two. But Churchill subsequently found out that they had come from Cleveland on Thursday afternoon, August 26, on the Little Miami Railroad and were already in the city.

Learning that the "boys" were planning to take a train on Thursday evening to New Richmond and then to Ripley, where they would cross the Ohio River into Mason County, the officers sprang into action. "An arrangement was…made with a city Hackman to drive to the depot, and when the pair of runaways came within hailing distance, he was to cry out, 'Here's a hack for New Richmond.'"[309] They fell for the ploy.

For several blocks, Churchill and his companions followed them in another hack until they reached the corner of Congress and Pike Streets. At a prearranged signal, the driver of the first hack stopped. The officers threw open the doors of the vehicle, hopped in and handcuffed the two men before they had a chance to draw their own weapons.

"The Marshal and his assistants jumped out of their hack, got into the one that contained the fugitives, and ordered the driver to drive them to Marshal Lewis W. Sifford's office, on the corner of Fourth and Vine streets."[310] Sifford had been appointed U.S. marshal for the Southern District of Ohio on March 13, 1857.

After taking the prisoners to the U.S. Custom House, Ingram demanded that Commissioner Newhall give them a hearing at once. It was then between nine and ten o'clock in the evening. According to the *Cincinnati Commercial*, Newhall "objected to examining the case at that hour of night, but Mr. Ingram insisted upon his right to an immediate examination; whereupon Mr. Newhall acceded to the demand."[311]

Ingram "testified that the negroes were his slaves owing him service and labor, and was corroborated by Mr. Tabb and Mr. White, who had accompanied him from Mason county."[312] Not surprisingly, Newhall remanded the two men to Ingram, and they were bundled into a carriage,

"Come and Join Us Brothers": a recruiting poster inviting African Americans to join the Union forces. *Courtesy Wikipedia.*

taken to the ferry and hurried across the Ohio River to Covington, Kentucky, at about midnight and placed in jail. The next morning, they would return to their former residence by railroad.

Later, it emerged that a man named Brawdy was also entangled in the case. Apparently, the two prisoners said he had accompanied them from Detroit after his children, who lived in Cincinnati, recognized them. However, there was some question about whether he was planning to help them. Ingram, for one, doubted it and wrote a letter "to inform his persecutors of the true state of the facts, in order to save him from their tender mercies."[313] Perhaps he was the person who gave them up.

In at least one instance, a person of color claimed to be a fugitive slave when he wasn't in order to take advantage of some gullible abolitionists and their antipathy for slave catchers. Late in May 1858, a large "mulatto" named Dade escaped from the Michigan State Prison. A "desperate and determined" individual, Dade was said to be forty years old; five feet, ten and a half inches tall; and "very smart and very ugly."[314] He was serving his second sentence, having been pardoned once previously.[315]

One day, the prisoner attacked a couple of his keepers, shattering the arm of one with an iron bar and sustaining a broken arm himself. As a result, he was placed in heavy shackles and consigned to one of the two cells reserved for prisoners serving life sentences.

Nevertheless, Dade managed to cut off the restraints and tunnel through the stone wall. (He would later claim that it took him three days and nights with no tools but a knife.) After moving stones that weighed up to one hundred pounds each and breaking through heavy iron plate, Dade made his way into a workshop. He then constructed a ladder, which he used to scale the wall. Finally, around midnight, he stole a prison horse and rode off during a raging storm, discarding his prison clothing in the yard.

Three hours later, Dade's escape was discovered. But his trail was lost after ten miles, washed away by the rain. The following Sunday, he preached a sermon to a large audience—or so he later said. They took up a collection for him, contributing "a sufficient sum to enable him to buy a horse," the *Evening Star* reported.[316]

While making his way from Jackson, Michigan, to Sandusky, Ohio, Dade stole at least three other horses and sold one for cash. But he was finally apprehended by Officer Adams of Jackson, who consigned him to the local jail. However, after Dade claimed to be a fugitive slave, local abolitionists obtained a writ of habeas corpus and succeeded in gaining his release. He immediately left town, with Officer Adams following behind.

At Bellefontaine, Adams took him into custody again. This time, despite threats by the townspeople to lynch Adams and free Dade, the officer was able to send a telegram to Jackson to obtain "proof of the truth of his assertion that Dade was an escaped convict."[317] After several other officers arrived by train, Dade agreed to return to prison if they did not place him in irons. Otherwise, he would demand they obtain a requisition. Despite his propensity for escaping, he was successfully "taken back to his old quarters" in Jackson.[318]

On December 5, 1858, Dade escaped yet again by cutting through a six-inch-thick plank. It was believed he had outside help. Despite reports that he had been sighted in Detroit, disguised in women's clothing, the *Jackson Patriot* suggested he was probably masquerading as a fugitive slave among the Ohio abolitionists.

IN A LETTER TO the *Free South* newspaper, one J. McM. Simpson described an incident that occurred in Zanesville, Ohio, on November 2, 1858. "There was quite a stir among the colored population of this city yesterday and last night," he wrote, "on account of the appearance of some 'Southern Bloods,' in our city on Wednesday last."[319]

A band of slave catchers had arrived in town a week earlier in pursuit of seven slaves who had fled from their masters. Simpson said the men were "well acquainted with their business" and quickly had "[U.S.] Marshal Laughlan and other officers harnessed, and under lively operation, before the colored folks smelt the rat."[320]

Then, on the night of Saturday, October 30, about half a dozen men were observed passing back and forth in front of the house of Washington M. Parker, a Black man with a wife and three children. The men "were in such a hurry on their flight, that they could not stop to give the old man a friendly salutation."[321]

It was soon rumored that the slave hunters and the officers were going to ransack Parker's house, and on Tuesday night, "large groups of big stout black men were seen crossing the lower bridge, on their way to Parker's."[322] Forewarned, Parker prepared to meet them with thirteen guns.

However, the expected confrontation was averted. Instead, the slaveholders were holed up in the Stacy House, smoking cigars, while the officers, "(the poor servants of the Slave Power), were plowing through the deep mud—

over hills and valleys in torrents of rain, hunting—what?"[323] Apparently, their intended quarry, the seven fugitive slaves, was gone.

This may have been the same party of slaves—"six negroes (3 men, a woman, and her two daughters)"—who fled from Wood County, (West) Virginia during this same period.[324] They were assumed to be headed to Zanesville because the woman's husband lived there.

In conclusion, Simpson asked the question that was on the minds of many others: "What is the difference between Ohio being a Slave State [*sic*], and her giving the slaveholder power to hunt down, catch and hold his slaves in the State? For my part, I see none."[325]

An unknown number of free Blacks and, conceivably, free Whites were enslaved through misuse of the Fugitive Slave Act. Amos Timmons was nearly one of them. A man of color, Timmons was born and raised in Columbiana County, Ohio, not far from Salem. Sometime in December 1858, he hired on as a boat hand and traveled down the Ohio River. On reaching Memphis, Tennessee, he was "betrayed by some of his fellow servants into the hands of the Philistines"—that is to say, he was thrown in jail, charged with being a fugitive slave.[326]

Timmons was known to be an honest, industrious and, apparently, incautious individual, since he had left behind the paperwork required

The Battle of Gettysburg is considered the turning point in the Civil War. *Courtesy Wikipedia.*

to prove he was a free man. But Richard H. Garrigues, a local attorney, immediately forwarded the necessary documents to Memphis. Nevertheless, the *Cleveland Daily Leader* noted that "Timmons will be a lucky negro if they reach there before his white captors have disposed of his soul and body to pay for the costs of his imprisonment."[327]

On New Year's Day, the following description of Timmons was printed in a Memphis newspaper: "He is of brown color, will weigh about 180 pounds; about 6 feet high; aged about 35 [other sources say 26] years; has a scar on the back of his neck running up and down his neck; also a scar on his left thumb, one joint stiffened."[328]

As the *Boston Liberator* observed, "We suppose if [Timmons] ever has the good fortune to get out of the clutches of the vampire, he will not again throw himself into the monster's way."[329] However, the documents did arrive, and by January 26, 1859, Timmons had been freed from jail. Presumably, he was on his way back to Ohio.

During the decade following the passage of the Fugitive Slave Act, stealing Black children and selling them into slavery became a lucrative business. For a couple of morally bereft Cincinnati police officers named Slater and Leonard, it seemed like a quick way to make a buck. On Saturday evening, August 27, 1859, the duo snatched a Black youth named Butler off the streets.

According to the *Cleveland Daily Leader*, Butler told them he was a slave from Kentucky and wanted to return to his master. However, Butler claimed that the two officers "told him they wanted him, and he must make no noise."[330] They then took him to a "sawdust room" in an engine house and placed him in handcuffs, which would seem to have been unnecessary if he, in fact, he had asked to go back to his owner.[331]

After taking Butler down to the river, the officers signaled someone on the other bank. A skiff soon crossed over from the Kentucky side, manned by U.S. Deputy Marshal Clinton Butts. The officers placed the youth in the vessel, and Slater joined him for the return trip. On reaching the opposite bank, Slater and Butts escorted their prisoner to the Covington jail. But it turned out Butler was not a slave at all but a free resident of Cincinnati. Slater and Leonard had "fallen into" a trap that had been set for them.[332]

As the *Cincinnati Gazette* reported, the kidnappers were "greatly alarmed" by this turn of events and "did not rest until the boy was brought back to Cincinnati."[333] Slater, in particular, expressed much regret for his role in the affair. When word of what had transpired began to circulate, Butler was taken from the jail at midnight on Sunday and returned to his home.

On August 30, Mayor Richard M. Bishop of Cincinnati, a Democrat and future governor of Ohio, reviewed the charges against the two officers and decided to discharge Slater and suspend Leonard for ten days. Bishop, known as "Uncle Richard," was regarded as a conscientious man but not a particularly astute politician. Although Deputy Butts, who lost an arm during the Turner Riot three years earlier, was also implicated, he apparently was not disciplined. Instead, he went on to become Covington's first chief of police.

Chapter 15

WAS IT NECESSARY?

Some modern historians have questioned whether the Civil War was necessary to end slavery. In his book *America Aflame*, David Goldfield suggests that "there may have been other means to achieve that noble end. In fact, the United States was the only country to require a civil war in order to abolish slavery."[334] He deems this particular war the United States' greatest failure.

But Goldfield—who admits he is "anti-war, particularly the Civil War"— is judging the Civil War in part by the long struggle for racial equality that followed up to the present day.[335] He also minimizes the fact that the war was fought to preserve the Union as well. States had begun seceding even before Lincoln became president—and for a time, there was a real possibility that the South might win. Besides, Goldfield wasn't enslaved.

Thomas Fleming argued that the United States could have simply purchased the slaves from the slaveholders and set them free. It certainly would have been cheaper, if blood counts for anything. Revised estimates of the Civil War's death toll now approach 850,000 and could total 1 million if those who died prematurely over the next two decades are included.[336]

However, by economist Claudia Goldin's reckoning, "the cost of having the government buy all the slaves in the United States in 1860 would be about $2.7 billion."[337] Even if this was spread out over twenty-five years, the annual cost would have been three times the total federal expenditures during the same period, according to Roger L. Ransom—assuming there was the political will to do so.

A greenback issued on August 10, 1861, in order to finance the war. *Wikipedia.*

Fleming also believed that both the North and the South suffered from a "disease of the public mind" because they looked at slavery from a moral standpoint when they should have approached it from a practical one.[338] It was a phrase he borrowed from President James Buchanan's description of abolitionist John Brown. And, like Goldfield, he seemed to hold abolitionists in lower regard than slave owners for forcing the issue. Both Fleming and Goldfield argue that a political solution would have been possible if the evangelical fervor could have been tamped down.

In 1860, a year before the war began, the federal debt was about $64.8 million. The war would cost an estimated $5.2 billion—money the government didn't have. In order to pay for the war, Congress passed the Legal Tender Act of 1862, allowing the government to print paper money ("greenbacks") and also sell $500 million in bonds. Prior to that, each bank was authorized to print its own form of currency, providing it was backed by gold. When the government took over this responsibility, however, it was no longer obligated to back the greenbacks with gold for the simple reason that it couldn't. It didn't own enough gold.

The following year, Congress passed the National Bank Act, which also was designed to help finance the war. It created a nationwide banking system that loaned money to the government and also established a national system of currency: paper bills and coins. According to the U.S. Treasury Department, the federal debt had exploded to $2.6 billion by the time the war was over, more than forty times what it had been just five years before.

Other historians, such as Ulrich B. Phillips, an unapologetic apologist for the Old South, have claimed that slavery as an institution was about to collapse under its own weight. As he wrote in *American Negro Slavery*, "The slaveholding

The fears of White citizens were stoked by images such as "A Southern Legislature in the 'Carpet-Bagger' Days." *Authors' collection.*

régime kept money scarce, population sparse and land values accordingly low; it restricted the opportunities of many men of both races, and it kept many of the natural resources of the Southern country neglected."[339] Slavery, he believed, had reached an evolutionary dead end and was being left behind by the industrial revolution in the North. But that assumes slaves couldn't have been put to work in industry as well. History proves otherwise.

To this day, the United States and Haiti remain the only two countries that went to war to end slavery. But the Haitian Revolution, which cast off French colonial rule, differed in being a slave uprising—the largest since Spartacus tried and failed nearly two thousand years earlier.

An estimated twenty-one to forty-five million people—or one to two times the population of Florida—remain in some form of slavery in various parts of the world. In Bangladesh, China, India, North Korea, Pakistan, Russia, Uzbekistan—more than one hundred countries altogether—slavery still exists on a wide scale. As Grace Forrest, founding director of Walk Free, has observed, "Modern slavery permeates every aspect of our society. It is woven through our clothes, lights up our electronics, and seasons our food."[340] For many, their servitude differs little from that of the nineteenth century. And the likelihood that these slaves will ever gain their freedom is slim without intense pressure from the international community.

AT ABOUT NINE O'CLOCK on the night of October 12, 1859, Oliver Anderson was dragged from his house near Chillicothe by a Kentuckian and "two Ohio negro hunters."[341] They had knocked on his door and demanded to see him. Having retired to bed, Anderson insisted they tell him what they wanted. They replied that he had a set of stolen chairs in his house. He denied it, offering to show them the bill of sale. As soon as he opened the door, they attacked, beating him severely.

When Anderson's wife screamed for help, one of the kidnappers struck her and threatened to kill her if she didn't keep quiet. The kidnappers then placed him in the bottom of a wagon and covered him with hay. They also wanted to grab Anderson's two-year-old son as a hostage, but the child's mother scooped him up and ran out the back door, looking for help. But there were no other houses in the vicinity. When she finally reached her closest neighbor, it was too late to save her husband.

One of the kidnappers was U.S. Deputy Marshal George Baker, aided by police officer Michael Harley. They took their prisoner to Portsmouth and then to a farm near Maysville, Kentucky, where his owner was said to reside. As a ruse, the Kentuckian had himself handcuffed by his companions, who would claim that he was a counterfeiter they were taking to Kentucky on a requisition from the governor.

"Anderson had been a resident of [Chillicothe] four or five years, and was a quiet, inoffensive and industrious man," the *Holmes County Republican* reported. "That he was a free man there [was] but little doubt; but whether he was or not, his being kidnapped in this manner is a most damnable outrage."[342] But in truth, he wasn't a free man. Nevertheless, the incident greatly upset the citizens of "Chillicothe and a public meeting was held to denounce the outrage and adopt measures to bring the perpetrators to justice."[343]

Owing to the public outrage, Baker and Harley were soon arrested and bound over for trial. They were subsequently acquitted on the principle established in the *Prigg v. Pennsylvania* case that the master has a right to recapture his slave using all necessary force. Although separated from his family and placed in bondage, Anderson managed to escape three months later, accompanied by two other slaves, including his brother. The trio passed through Columbus on Friday, January 20, 1860, on their way to Canada.

MANY FUGITIVE SLAVES SETTLED near Sandusky, knowing that Canada—and freedom—was just a boat ride away. Two slave families, the I. Marshalls and the T. Burnetts, made their way to Sandusky in 1859. The former consisted of a husband, a wife and four children and the latter a husband,

The Democrats opposed Reconstruction, asserting the United States was a "White Man's Government." *Courtesy of Wikipedia.*

a wife and three children. The men took jobs working in the woods west of town, where James P. Gay and E. Merry had been contracted to clear timber. Each family was housed in one of the shacks that Gay and Merry built for their workers.

Given the remoteness of the location, the fugitives could have lived there in relative safety and obscurity. However, a man named Thomas Davis, who lived in the vicinity, learned about them and decided to turn them in for the reward that had been offered by the slaveholder.[344]

Through Davis's machinations, the slaveholders and their agents seized the Marshalls and the Burnetts one evening and carried them to the Sandusky, Dayton & Cincinnati Railroad two miles away. Hearing their cries for help, Louis and Palmer Pruitt, who lived nearby, rushed to their assistance. Although Louis shot one of the kidnappers, "as the blood tracks showed the next morning, the Pruitts alone, unassisted could not cope with the superior arms and numbers of the slave catchers who succeeded in getting away with their prey."[345] But they did leave behind a two-year-old child, who was found a day later.

As quickly as they could, the Pruitts assembled a posse, which rushed to Castalia in hopes of intercepting the train. But it departed before they were able to board it. According to the Pruitts, the kidnappers continued on to a point near Venice, where the train made an unscheduled stop in the middle of the night. They then took their captives to an extra passenger car that had been added to the train and rode it all the way to Kentucky, where they arrived the next morning. As far as is known, railroad officials never explained why they assisted the slave hunters in this manner, but the law was on their side.

Some years later after slavery had been abolished, the father of the child who had been left behind returned for it and took it back to Maysville, Kentucky, with him. Whether the mother survived is unknown.

THE *CINCINNATI GAZETTE* REPORTED that an attempt had been made on May 28, 1860, to kidnap a free Black man and sell him into slavery. Jeremiah Johnson, who was White, approached James Upson in Cincinnati and offered him a job working on the river—a common ploy. Upson agreed and accompanied Johnson to the Walnut Street ferry landing.

When they reached the river, Johnson told him that he was going to work as a hand on the ferry boat and urged him to go aboard. Upson refused. Johnson then "seized him by the neck, pointed a revolver in his

D.W. Griffith's epic pro–Ku Klux Klan film, *The Birth of a Nation*, helped spur the organization's rebirth in 1915. *Courtesy of Wikipedia.*

face, and told him that if he showed the slightest resistance he would blow his brains out."[346]

Upson immediately began screaming bloody murder, and a large crowd quickly assembled. Johnson offered twenty dollars to anyone who would help him transport the "fugitive slave" across the river to Kentucky. Meanwhile, the Black man "piteously" begged the crowd to rescue him, insisting that he had never been a slave.

At that moment, "two gentlemen passed along the levee in a carriage, one of whom shouted to Johnson to let the negro go, whereupon Johnson called them d—d abolitionists, with other insulting language."[347] Leaping from their carriage, the men grabbed Johnson by the hair, dragged him to the ground and began striking him.

Fortunately for Johnson, Officers Colby, Chumley and Brockington of the river police came running. After rescuing Johnson from his assailants, they hauled him off to the Hammond Street police station, where he was charged with kidnapping.

WHATEVER POSSESSED A TWELVE-YEAR-OLD boy to step off the boat onto the Cincinnati landing will never be known. Perhaps he was urged to do so by one of the free Blacks who lived and worked along the riverfront in "Little Africa" (also called Bucktown). Maybe he was persuaded by one of the city's many abolitionists. Or, possibly, he acted on impulse. But in doing so, young Henson stepped into the pages of history, if only in a small way.

About the second week of October 1860, Henson was traveling down the Ohio River with his master, Lewis Bruce. They were relocating from Bruce's former residence in Virginia to a new home in Missouri. Bruce would later claim that the boat tied up to the Cincinnati shore against his wishes, although it is likely that the stop was always on the vessel's itinerary.

When Henson was subsequently "found" within the jurisdiction of the State of Ohio, David Gibbs filed a writ of habeas corpus, and John J. Jolliffe was engaged to represent the boy in court. Jolliffe argued that since the boy was now standing on free ground, he must be granted his freedom. Slavery could not, he insisted, exist under the constitution and laws of Ohio. It was not the first time he'd made this argument.

Countering Jolliffe's position was the assertion by opposing counsel that "while we should carefully maintain our own rights, yet the courts must also see to it that the rights of our neighbors were not infringed."[348] The Ohio Supreme Court, under Republican Judge William Gholson (joined by Judges Carter, Mallon and Collins) agreed. Their reasoning was:

> *Although the jurisdiction of our courts extended for many purposes to boats on the Ohio river, the citizens of Virginia and other States bordering on the south had a right to the free navigation of the river; that the stopping of boats and tying up at the landing was a necessary incident to the right of free navigation, and as such, rested on a higher basis than the mere jurisdiction of the river.*[349]

As a slave, Henson was a citizen of neither Ohio nor Virginia. He was simply property. Therefore, the sheriff was ordered to return him to his owner, the same as if he had been a runaway horse.

EDWARD VANSICKLE, A BLACK man, was on board the *Collier*, a mail boat moored at the Cincinnati wharf, on Christmas Day 1860 when he was arrested by Deputy U.S. Marshal William L. Manson. A warrant had been sworn out by R.M. Moore, agent for the trustees of the estate of the late

Eli Vansickle. It charged that the thirty-seven-year-old "boy" was a slave who had run off from his master's plantation in Louisville, Kentucky, some eighteen months earlier. Eventually, he found work on the steamer.

Despite an alleged addiction to alcohol, Vansickle was regarded as a valuable commodity. As soon as he was taken into custody, he was hauled before U.S. Commissioner Thomas Powell and, a few minutes later, placed in a Covington jail after proof of his ownership was presented. It was expected that he would be returned to Louisville the next morning and then "disposed of down South."[350]

As the *Cincinnati Gazette* noted:

> *In this case, the anxious politicians of the country may see with what alacrity the Fugitive Slave Law is executed by the citizens of Ohio. This case is a fair illustration of the majority that have occurred during the past three years, as, during this time, not a colored person arrested on a warrant of a United States Commissioner has been set free again or rescued.*[351]

It had been ten years since the Fugitive Slave Act was passed. During the interim, far more Blacks were re-enslaved than successfully escaped—and just not re-enslaved. According to the American Anti-Slavery Society, "The number of ACTUALLY FREE persons, STOLEN, KIDNAPPED from the Northern States, and, in utter defiance of law and justice alike, HURRIED INTO SLAVERY, is to be reckoned by hundreds."[352]

But by the end of the war, give or take a few months, all formerly enslaved persons were free, save in the Indian territories. That would require four separate treaties in 1866 with the Cherokee, Creek, Seminole and Chickasaw-Choctaw tribes. However, free Blacks still weren't free to vote, own land, work for themselves and even use public accommodations. Those rights were not granted until the passage of the Fourteenth Amendment to the Constitution in 1868. And keeping those rights would necessitate a long struggle of another sort, culminating in the civil rights movement a century later.

NOTES

Introduction

1. Coffin, *Reminiscences*, 25
2. Douglass, *Narrative*, 101.
3. Ibid.
4. By purchasing Douglass's freedom, they were, in effect, becoming slave owners, if only briefly.
5. King, *Ohio: First Fruits*, 376.
6. Between this book and that, we have covered most of Ohio's significant UGRR stories.
7. Cairnes, *Slave Power*, 90.
8. Schulz, "Perilous Lure."
9. Blight, *Race and Reunion*, 298.
10. Ibid.
11. Ibid., 299.
12. Mosby, letter to Sam Chapman.

Chapter 1

13. Sloane, "Underground Railroad of the Firelands."
14. *Liberator*, "Friend of Man."
15. Shane, "How the Underground Railroad Got Its Name."
16. Ibid.
17. Shane, *Flee North*.

18. *Evening Post*, "Specimen of Abolitionism."
19. Torrey would go to prison for his UGRR activities, while Smallwood moved to Canada to avoid prosecution.
20. *Green-Mountain Freeman*, "Whig Party."
21. Ohio Memory, "Underground Railway of the Lake Country of Western New York."
22. Gara, *Liberty Line*, 42.
23. In his 1996 preface, Gara stated he was "naïve" when he originally wrote the book thirty years earlier and should have given more acknowledgement to the work of White abolitionists.
24. Kitt, "Advertisement."
25. They marked the trees at the corners of their claim with their initials.
26. Burke, "Ohio Valley's First Fugitive Slave."
27. Ibid.
28. Ibid.
29. Ibid.
30. Evans, *History of Adams County*, 583.
31. In today's dollars, this would be nearly $7,000.
32. Evans, *History of Adams County*, 584.
33. Ibid. 584.
34. Sloane, "Underground Railroad of the Firelands."

Chapter 2

35. Parker, *His Promised Land*, 85.
36. Ibid., 86.
37. Siebert Collection, "Elijah Huftelen's."
38. Williams, "Underground Railroad Signals."
39. Ibid.
40. Ibid.
41. Meyers, *Historic Black Settlements*, 43–47.
42. Keyes, "Unsung Naturalist."
43. Bradford, *Scenes in the Life*, 57.
44. Likely North Bloomfield.
45. Howe, *Historical Collections of Ohio*, 346.
46. Ibid., 663.
47. Ibid.
48. Siebert, "Quaker Section."
49. Ibid.
50. *Liberator*, "Specimen of Slavery."
51. Middleton, *Black Laws*, 96.

52. *Liberator*, "Specimen of Slavery."
53. Harrold, *Border War*, 80.
54. Coffin, *Reminiscences*, 63.
55. Ibid., 348.

Chapter 3

56. Schneider, "Guthrie Home in Putnam."
57. Ibid.
58. Ibid.
59. Schneider, "Escaping Slaves Found Refuge."
60. Ibid.
61. Buckingham, *Solomon Sturges*, 46.
62. Schneider, "Escaping Slaves Found Refuge."
63. Harrold, *Border War*, 101.
64. Meyers, *Historic Black Settlements*, 25–33.
65. Harrold, *Border War*, 102.
66. *Liberator*, "Affairs in Ohio."
67. *Democrat and Herald*, "Abolition Riot."
68. Ibid.
69. Harrold, *Border War*, 102.
70. Hagedorn, *Beyond the River*, 187.
71. Ibid., 187.
72. *Liberator*, "Affairs in Ohio."
73. *Weekly Mississippian*, "Progress of Whiggery."
74. Payerchin, "Details Emerge."
75. Clarke and Clarke, *Narratives of the Sufferings*, 84.
76. *Liberator*, "Jail Breaking at Elyria."
77. Sloane, "Underground Railroad of the Firelands."
78. Coffin, *Reminiscences*, 263.
79. Sloane, "Underground Railroad of the Firelands."

Chapter 4

80. M. Jones, "Interview with Fannie Moore."
81. Murray, "Giles R. Wright, Jr."
82. Wright, "Hidden in Plain View."
83. Stukin, "Unraveling the Myth."
84. Clarke and Clarke, *Narratives of the Sufferings*, 84.
85. Ibid.
86. *History of Geauga and Lake Counties*, 25.

87. Ibid., 25.
88. Clarke and Clarke, *Narratives of the Sufferings*, 96.
89. Ibid. 96.
90. *History of Geauga and Lake Counties*, 26.
91. Ibid., 26.
92. Ibid., 26.
93. Clarke and Clarke, *Narratives of the Sufferings*, 86.
94. Ibid.
95. Ibid.
96. Ibid.
97. Ibid., 87.
98. Ibid.
99. Ibid.
100. Ibid., 88.
101. Ibid.

Chapter 5

102. Perrin, *History of Stark County*, 374.
103. Ibid.
104. Ibid.
105. Massillon Public Library, "George Duncan Letter."
106. *New York Times*, "Abolitionists."
107. *Democratic Standard*, "From the Ohio Sun."
108. Ibid.
109. Ibid.
110. Snodgrass, *Underground Railroad*.
111. Pollitt, *Antislavery Movement*, 56.
112. Mitchell, *Under-Ground Railroad*, 17.
113. Ibid., 27.
114. Ibid.
115. *Cincinnati Enquirer*, "Another Exposé."
116. Grieve, *Centennial History of Cincinnati*, 759.
117. Ibid.
118. *Richmond Enquirer*, "Abolition Riot at Cincinnati."
119. Coffin, *Reminiscences*, 541.
120. Ohio History Connection, "N.B. Sisson's Letter."
121. Many homes had such cellars, often accessed through a door in the kitchen floor.
122. Ohio History Connection, "N.B. Sisson's Letter,"

Chapter 6

123. Sherrod, "Secret Life."
124. Howard, "New Light Is Shed."
125. West, interview.
126. Skeptics, "Lawn Jockey Statues."
127. Ibid.
128. Landers, "Story of Groomsman Statue."
129. *Marietta Intelligencer*, February 11, 1847.
130. Ibid.
131. Ibid.
132. *Marietta Times*, "Businessman/Abolitionist Died."
133. *History of Geauga and Lake Counties*, 25.
134. Ibid.
135. Ibid.
136. Ibid.
137. *Daily Union*, "Letter from Ex-Governor."
138. Ibid.
139. Ibid.
140. *Daily Union*, "Letter from Ex-Governor."
141. *Daily Union*, January 21, 1851.
142. Ibid.
143. *Daily Union*, "Letter from Ex-Governor."
144. "Governor Joseph Desha."

Chapter 7

145. Lucas, interview by W.H. Siebert.
146. Ibid.
147. Hise, *Daniel Howell Hise*, 21.
148. Ibid., 22.
149. Ibid., 35.
150. Ibid., 56.
151. Galbreath, "Anti-Slavery Movement."
152. Ibid.
153. Ibid.
154. Hise, *Daniel Howell Hise*, 229.
155. Ibid., 267.
156. Swetye, "Local Historians."
157. Dickinson, *History of Belpre*, 132.
158. Ibid.

159. Ibid., 133.
160. Troy, *Hair-Breadth Escapes*, 100.
161. Ibid., 101.
162. Ibid.
163. May, *Fugitive Slave Law*, 11.
164. *Daily Union*, "Letter from Ex-Governor."
165. *Sunbury American*, "Slave Case in Cleveland."
166. Ibid.
167. Ibid.
168. Ibid.

Chapter 8

169. B. Williams, *History of Clermont and Brown Counties*, 400.
170. *Pittsburgh Gazette*, "Mob Law Triumphant!"
171. *Perry County Democrat*, "Brown County, Ohio."
172. *Pittsburgh Gazette*, "Mob Law Triumphant!"
173. *Brooklyn Daily Eagle*, "Riot in Ohio."
174. Ibid.
175. *Liberator*, December 20, 1844.
176. *Democratic Standard*, December 31, 1844.
177. *Brooklyn Daily Eagle*, "Hoax."
178. *Tennessean*, "Hoax."
179. *Daily American Telegraph*, September 29, 1852.
180. Sloane, "Underground Railroad of the Firelands."
181. *Hampshire Advertiser*, "Slave Mother."
182. Sloane, "Underground Railroad of the Firelands."
183. *Buffalo (NY) Express and Illustrated Buffalo Express*, "Attempt to Arrest."
184. Padden, "Underground Railroad Reminiscences."
185. Ibid.
186. Sloane, "Underground Railroad of the Firelands."
187. *Buffalo (NY) Express and Illustrated Buffalo Express*, "Attempt to Arrest."
188. Sloane, "Underground Railroad of the Firelands."
189. *Weekly Commercial*, "Escape of Fugitive Slaves."
190. *Times-Picayune*, "Sarah Haynes."
191. Randolph, *Reports of Cases Argued*, 32.
192. *Green-Mountain Freeman*, "Retribution at Last."
193. *Green-Mountain Freeman*, March 5, 1879.

Chapter 9

194. Burroughs, *Riverby*, 174.

195. Visit Baton Rouge, "Myrtles Plantation."
196. Taylor, "Debunking the 'History.'"
197. Albrecht, "Families Linked."
198. Ibid.
199. Ibid.
200. Dix, "Underground Railroad."
201. Denton, "19th-Century Henrico County Records."
202. William Shakespeare's wife, Anne Hathaway, inherited only his second-best bed.
203. Doran, "Caroline Brown House."
204. *Ohio Star*, "Serious Affray."
205. Ibid.
206. May, *Fugitive Slave Law*, 28.
207. King, who never married or had any children, is alleged by some to have been the lover of President James Buchanan, with whom he lived for the last thirteen years of his life.
208. Coffin, *Reminiscences*, 338.
209. *Liberator*, "Another Remarkable Escape."
210. Coffin, *Reminiscences*, 340.

Chapter 10

211. Bresler, "Follow the Drinking Gourd."
212. Ibid.
213. Ibid.
214. May, *Fugitive Slave Law*, 38.
215. Ibid., 38.
216. *National Era*, "Slave Kidnapper Convicted."
217. Ibid.
218. May, *Fugitive Slave Law*, 38.
219. *Weekly Marysville Tribune*, "Attempt to Kidnap—Murder."
220. May, *Fugitive Slave Law*, 38.
221. *National Era*, "Slave Kidnapper Convicted."
222. *Green-Mountain Freeman*, "Kidnapping in Ohio."
223. Ibid.
224. Ibid.
225. *Herald of Freedom*, "Horrid Murder of a Colored Man."
226. May, *Fugitive Slave Law*, 39.
227. *Louisville Daily Courier*, "Capture of Runaway Slaves."
228. *South-Western*, "Fugitive Slave Captured."
229. *Louisville Daily Courier*, "Capture of Runaway Slaves."

230. Ibid.
231. *New Orleans Crescent*, "Kidnapping."
232. Ibid.
233. *Buffalo (NY) Morning Express and Illustrated Buffalo Express*, "Kidnapping."
234. *New Orleans Crescent*, "Kidnapping."
235. Ibid.
236. *Washington Union*, "Doing Unto Others."
237. *New England Farmer*, "Kidnapping of Free Negroes."
238. Coleman, *Slavery Times in Kentucky*, 212.

Chapter 11

239. Brown, "Benjamin R. Hanby."
240. Ibid.
241. *Piqua Dail Call*, "Darling Nellie Gray."
242. *Lancaster Eagle-Gazette*, "Village of Rushville Claims."
243. Drew, *North-Side View*, 362.
244. *National Era*, "Letter from Cincinnati."
245. Drew, *North-Side View*, 364.
246. Ibid.
247. Ibid., 365.
248. Ibid.
249. Ibid., 364.
250. Troy, *Hair-Breadth Escapes*, 11.
251. Mitchell, *Under-Ground Railroad*, 31.
252. May, *Fugitive Slave Law*, 83.
253. Ibid.
254. *Liberator*, "Harboring Slaves."
255. Ibid.
256. *Anti-Slavery Bugle*, "Kidnapper Caught."

Chapter 12

257. More recently, they are given ghost stories.
258. Ohio History Connection, "Boris M. Risley's Statement."
259. Gallick, "County's Efforts Not Forgotten."
260. J. Jones, "Secret Room Found."
261. *Columbus Dispatch*, "Station of 'Underground Railway.'"
262. Quick, "Hole in Wall of Cellar."
263. Ibid.
264. Ibid.

265. *Circleville Herald*, "Old Tunnel in City Stirs Up Aged Legends."
266. Ibid.
267. Ibid.
268. *Cincinnati Times-Star*, "Underground Chamber Found."
269. *Dayton Daily News*, "Underground Room Still Mystery."
270. Fruehling and Smith, "Subterranean Hideaways."
271. Troy, *Hair-Breadth Escapes*, 42.
272. Ibid., 42.
273. Trowbridge, *Ferry Boy and the Financier*, 318.
274. Meyers and Walker, *Reverse Underground Railroad in Ohio*, 110.
275. Ibid., 100.
276. *Liberator*, "Two Runaways Taken."
277. *Liberator*, "Kidnappers Arrested."
278. Ibid.

Chapter 13

279. Michener, "Willis, Uncle Wallace and Aunt Minerva."
280. Ibid.
281. Ward, *Dark Midnight When I Rise*, 406.
282. Ibid., 139.
283. Ibid., 110.
284. Larson, *Bound for the Promised Land*, 101.
285. May, *Fugitive Slave Law*, 84–85.
286. Ibid., 84.
287. Ibid., 85.
288. Ibid.
289. *Daily Delta*, "Regular Case of Kidnapping."
290. Ibid.
291. Ibid.
292. *Anti-Slavery Bugle*, "Van Tuyl, the Kidnapper."
293. *Quad-City Times*, "Cincinnati Slave Case."
294. Ibid.
295. *Liberator*, "Subjugation of Ohio."
296. Ibid.
297. Ibid.
298. *Anti-Slavery Bugle*, "Late Slave Case."
299. Ibid.
300. Ibid.

Chapter 14

301. Sloane, "Underground Railroad of the Firelands."
302. Gates, "Who Really Ran the Underground Railroad."
303. National Park Service, "Interpreting the Underground Railroad."
304. Pogue, "Underground Railroad Signals."
305. Siebert, *Underground Railroad*, 346.
306. Lennon, "Slave Escapes, Prices."
307. *Cleveland Morning Leader*, "Capture by U.S. Official Bloodhounds."
308. Ibid.
309. *Liberator*, "Arrest of Fugitives."
310. *Weekly Advertiser*, "Two Slaves Escaped."
311. *Cincinnati Commercial*, August 28, 1858.
312. *Cleveland Morning Leader*, "Capture by U.S. Official Bloodhounds."
313. *Detroit Free Press*, "New Phase of the Brawdy Case."
314. *Hillsdale Standard*, "Escape."
315. *Evansville Daily Journal*, "Desperado at Large."
316. *Evening Star*, "Slippery Negro."
317. Ibid.
318. Ibid.
319. *Liberator*, "Nigger Hunters About!"
320. Ibid.
321. Ibid.
322. Ibid.
323. Ibid.
324. *Union*, "More Runaways."
325. *Liberator*, "Nigger Hunters About!"
326. *Western Reserve Chronicle*, "Salam [*sic*] Republican says."
327. *Cleveland Daily Leader*, "Outrage."
328. *Memphis Daily Appeal*, "Jailor's Notice."
329. *Liberator*, "Final Correction."
330. *Cleveland Daily Leader*, "Kidnapping Case in Cincinnati."
331. *Raftsman's Journal*, September 7, 1859.
332. May, *Fugitive Slave Law*, 124.
333. Ibid.

Chapter 15

334. Goldfield, *America Aflame*, 3.
335. Ibid.

336. The higher figure would mean that one person died in the Civil War for every four slaves freed.

337. Ransom, "Economics of the Civil War."

338. Fleming, *Disease of the Public Mind*, xiv.

339. Phillips, *American Negro Slavery*, 401.

340. Reliefweb, "Global Slavery Index 2023."

341. *Cleveland Daily Leader*, "Kidnapping No Crime."

342. *Holmes County Republican*, "Another Infernal Outrage."

343. *Highland Weekly News*, "Kidnapping in Chillicothe."

344. Not to be confused with Thomas R. Davis, who was a friend to local African Americans.

345. Sloane, "Underground Railroad of the Firelands."

346. *Cincinnati Gazette*, May 29, 1860.

347. Ibid.

348. *Anti-Slavery Bugle*, "Jurisdiction of Ohio."

349. Ibid.

350. *Cincinnati Daily Press*, "Taken Down South."

351. *Civilian and Gazette Weekly*, "Another Fugitive Slave Surrendered."

352. May, *Fugitive Slave Law*, 161.

BIBLIOGRAPHY

Articles

Albrecht, Robert. "Families Linked Through Vintage Photos." *Columbus (OH) Dispatch,* January 31, 1996.
Anti-Slavery Bugle (Lisbon, OH). "The Jurisdiction of Ohio." October 27, 1860.
———. "Kidnapper Caught—Two Boys From Cincinnati Recovered." March 22, 1856.
———. "The Late Slave Case in Cincinnati." November 14, 1857.
———. "Van Tuyl, the Kidnapper, Given Up by the Authorities of Kentucky." April 10, 1858.
———. "Washington's Runaway Slave." August 22, 1845.
Baumgardner, Alice. "When the Enslaved Went South." *New Yorker*, November 19, 2020.
Bresler, Joel. "Follow the Drinking Gourd: A Cultural History." http://www.followthedrinkinggourd.org.
Brooklyn (NY) Daily Eagle. "A Hoax." December 23, 1844.
———. "Riot in Ohio." December 17, 1844.
Brown, Clarence J. "Benjamin R. Hanby." In *Appendix, Congressional Record*. Government Printing Office, 1965.
Bryant, Brooks, and Emily Brammer. "The Fee Brothers." Clio, July 24, 2018. https://www.theclio.com.
Buffalo (NY) Express and Illustrated Buffalo Express. "Attempt to Arrest Fugitive Slaves in Ohio." November 6, 1852.
Buffalo (NY) Morning Express and Illustrated Buffalo Express. "Kidnapping." November 20, 1854.

Burke, Henry. "The Ohio Valley's First Fugitive Slave." *River Jordan* (blog), June 1, 2011. http://henryrburke.blogspot.com.

Cincinnati (OH) Daily Press. "Romantic." December 9, 1861.

———. "Taken Down South." December 27, 1860.

Cincinnati (OH) Enquirer. "Another Exposé." August 5, 1843.

Cincinnati (OH) Times-Star. "Underground Chamber Found; Believed Once Slave Hideout." October 20, 1949.

Circleville (OH) Herald. "Old Tunnel in City Stirs Up Aged Legends." May 28, 1947.

Civilian and Gazette Weekly (Galveston, TX). "Another Fugitive Slave Surrendered." January 15, 1861.

Cleveland (OH) Daily Leader. "Kidnapping Case in Cincinnati." September 1, 1859.

———. "Kidnapping No Crime." December 20, 1859.

———. "Outrage on a Free Colored Man." December 24, 1858.

Cleveland (OH) Morning Leader. "Capture by U.S. Official Bloodhounds." August 30, 1858.

Columbus (OH) Dispatch. "Station of 'Underground Railway' Still Stands in East Side." May 28, 1925.

Daily Delta (New Orleans, LA). "Regular Case of Kidnapping." December 25, 1857.

Daily Union (Washington, D.C.). "Letter from Ex-Governor Metcalfe of Kentucky." January 21, 1851.

———. Untitled article. January 21, 1851.

Dayton (OH) Daily News. "Underground Room Still Mystery in Richland Co." November 6, 1949.

Democrat and Herald (Wilmington, OH). "Abolition Riot." May 2, 1839.

Democratic Standard (Georgetown, OH). "From the Ohio Sun." December 6, 1842.

Denton, Lisa. "19th-Century Henrico County Records Offer Clues on the Lives of Free Black Individuals." UncommonWealth, May 25, 2022. https:// uncommonwealth.virginiamemory.com.

Detroit (MI) Free Press. "New Phase of the Brawdy Case." September 18, 1858.

Dix, Paula. "Underground Railroad Part of House History." *Ohio State Lantern*, October 23, 1979.

Doran, Matt. "The Caroline Brown House." *Teaching Columbus* (blog), February 6, 2014. https://www.teachingcolumbus.org.

Evansville (IN) Daily Journal. "A Desperado at Large." June 2, 1858.

Evening Post (New York, NY). "Specimen of Abolitionism." September 23, 1842.

Evening Star (Washington, D.C.). "Slippery Negro." June 10, 1858.

Fruehling, Byron D., and Robert H. Smith. "Subterranean Hideaways of the Underground Railroad in Ohio: An Architectural, Archaeological and Historical Critique of Local Traditions." *Ohio History Journal* 102 (Summer– Autumn 1993).

Galbreath, C.B. "Anti-Slavery Movement in Columbiana County." *Ohio Archaeological and Historical Publications* 30 (1921).

Gallick, Thomas. "Underground Railroad: County's Efforts Not Forgotten." *ThisWeek Community News* (Columbus, OH), February 15, 2018.

Gates, Henry Louis, Jr. "Who Really Ran the Underground Railroad?" PBS. https://www.pbs.org.

"Governor Joseph Desha." In *Register of the Kentucky State Historical Society* (George G. Fetter, 1904).

Green-Mountain Freeman (Montpelier, VT). "Kidnapping in Ohio. Horrible Murder of a Free Colored Man." June 22, 1854.

———. "Retribution at Last." April 24, 1878.

———. "The Whig Party." December 6, 1844.

Hampshire Advertiser (Southampton, England). "The Slave Mother." December 25, 1852.

Herald of Freedom (Wilmington, OH). "Horrid Murder of a Colored Man." June 2, 1854.

Highland (County, OH) Weekly News. "Kidnapping in Chillicothe." October 27, 1859.

Hillsdale (MI) Standard. "An Escape." May 25, 1858.

Holmes County (OH) Republican. "Another Infernal Outrage." November 3, 1859.

Howard, Jack. "New Light Is Shed on Parts Played by Springfield and County in Underground Railroad of Century Ago." *News-Sun* (Springfield, OH), November 20, 1949.

Jones, Johnny. "Secret Room Found Under Home." *Columbus (OH) Dispatch*, March 15, 1954.

Jones, Marjorie. "Interview with Fannie Moore, Ex-Slave." In *Slave Narratives*, Works Projects Administration (Washington, D.C.: Library of Congress, 1941).

Keyes, Allison. "Harriet Tubman, an Unsung Naturalist." *Audubon Magazine*, February 25, 2020.

Kitt, Frederick. "Advertisement." *Pennsylvania Gazette and Universal Daily Advertiser*, May 24, 1796.

Lancaster (OH) Eagle-Gazette. "Village of Rushville Claims 'Darling Nellie Gray.'" December 27, 1934.

Landers, Ann. "Story of Groomsman Statue Is Myth." *Gettysburg (PA) Times*, November 3, 1982.

Lennon, Conor. "Slave Escapes, Prices, and the Fugitive Slave Act of 1850." *Journal of Law and Economics* 59, no. 3 (August 1, 2016).

Liberator (Boston, MA). "Affairs in Ohio." June 14, 1839.

———. "Another Remarkable Escape." February 4, 1853.

———. "Arrest of Fugitives." September 10, 1858.

———. "A Final Correction." December 31, 1858.

———. "From the Friend of Man." October 11, 1839.

———. "Harboring Slaves." November 27, 1857.

———. "Jail Breaking at Elyria." April 23, 1841.

———. "The Kidnappers Arrested." December 4, 1857.

———. "Nigger Hunters About!" December 10, 1858.

———. "A Specimen of Slavery." April 20, 1838.

———. "The Subjugation of Ohio." November 27, 1857.

———. "Two Runaways Taken at Cleveland." November 27, 1857.

———. "The Under-Ground Rail-Road." December 20, 1844.

Louisville (KY) Daily Courier. "Capture of Runaway Slaves." September 30, 1854.

Lucas, Geo. W.S. Interviewed by W.H. Siebert, Salem, Ohio, August 14, 1892.

Marietta (OH) Times. "Businessman/Abolitionist Died 122 Years Ago This Week." January 20, 2014.

Massillon Public Library. "George Duncan Letter to Thomas Rotch." Massillon Memory. https://ohiomemory.org.

Memphis (TN) Daily Appeal. "Jailor's Notice." January 1, 1859.

Michener, Judith. "Willis, Uncle Wallace and Aunt Minerva." Encyclopedia of Oklahoma History and Culture. https://www.okhistory.org.

Mosby, John S. Letter to Sam Chapman. May 9, 1907. Gilder Lehrman Institute of American History. https://www.gilderlehrman.org.

Murray, Brian T. "Giles R. Wright, Jr., Renowned Scholar of African American History, Dies at 73." *Star Ledger* (Newark, NY), February 5, 2009.

Myrtles Plantation. "The Legend of Chloe & Other Ghost Stories." https://www.myrtlesplantation.com.

National Era (Washington, D.C.). "Letter from Cincinnati." September 16, 1852.

———. "A Slave Kidnapper Convicted of Manslaughter—Conviction of McCord." December 7, 1854.

National Park Service. "Research and Interpreting the Underground Railroad." https://www.nps.gov.

New England Farmer (Boston, MA). "Kidnapping of Free Negroes." December 2, 1854.

New Orleans (LA) Crescent. "Kidnapping." November 29, 1854.

News-Journal (Hillsboro, OH). "A Black Christmas." December 29, 1887.

New York Times. "The Abolitionists." January 6, 1906.

Ohio History Connection. "Boris M. Risley's Statement to Wilbur Siebert, Sept. 1945." Wilbur H. Siebert Underground Railroad Collection. https://www.ohiomemory.org.

———. "Elijah Huftelen's The Underground Railroad." Wilbur H. Siebert Underground Railroad Collection. https://www.ohiomemory.org.

———. "N.B. Sisson's Letter to Wilbur Siebert, Sept. 16, 1894.:

Ohio Memory. "The Underground Railway of the Lake Country of Western New York." Wilbur H. Siebert Underground Railroad Collection. https://www.

ohiomemory.org. Wilbur H. Siebert Underground Railroad Collection. https://www.ohiomemory.org.

Ohio Star (Ravenna). "Serious Affray Between a Party of Fugitive Slaves and Their Pursuers." August 3, 1853.

Padden, H.F. "Underground Railroad Reminiscences." *Firelands Pioneer*, New Series, 5 (July 1888).

Payerchin, Richard. "Details Emerge of Oberlin Slave Rescue." *Morning Journal*, (Oberlin, OH), April 2, 2016. https://www.morningjournal.com.

Perry County (PA) Democrat. "In Brown County, Ohio, Between Kentuckians and Citizens of Ohio—Several Persons Killed—Houses Burnt—Military Collected to Arrest the Rioters!" December 26, 1844.

Piqua (OH) Dail Call. "Story of How Song 'Darling Nellie Gray' Was Written Is Told Piquad by Ohioan Who is Noted Historian." June 17, 1931.

Pittsburgh (PA) Gazette. "Mob Law Triumphant!" December 21, 1844.

Pogue, Marcia Baker. "Underground Railroad Signals." *Ohio Southland* 6, no. 12 (1995).

Quad-City Times (Davenport, IA). "The Cincinnati Slave Case." December 3, 1857.

Quick, Paul D. "Hole in Wall of Cellar Discloses Old Slave Route." *Columbus (OH) Citizen*, May 26, 1947.

Ransom, Roger L. "The Economics of the Civil War." EH.net. https://eh.net.

Reliefweb. "The Global Slavery Index 2023." https://reliefweb.int.

Richmond (VA) Enquirer. "Abolition Riot at Cincinnati." August 11, 1843.

Schneider, Norris F. "Escaping Slaves Found Refuge in Region." *Times-Recorder* (Zanesville, OH), February 6, 1983.

———. "Guthrie Home in Putnam Serves as 'Underground Railroad' Stop." *Times Recorder* (Zanesville, OH), February 4, 1973.

Schulz, Kathryn. "The Perilous Lure of the Underground Railroad." *New Yorker*, August 22, 2016.

Shane, Scott. "How the Underground Railroad Got Its Name." *New York Times*, September 11, 2023.

Sherrod, Pamela. "The Secret Life of the Black Lawn Jockey." *Chicago Tribune*, February 8, 1988.

Siebert, Wilbur H. "A Quaker Section of the Underground Railroad in Northern Ohio." *Ohio History Journal* (1930).

Skeptics. "Were Lawn Jockey Statues Used to Indicate Stops on the Underground Railroad?" https://skeptics.stackexchange.com

Sloane, Rush R. "The Underground Railroad of the Firelands." *Firelands Pioneer* 5 (July 1888).

Southern Press (Washington, D.C.). "Attempt to Arrest a Fugitive Slave." June 14, 1851.

South-Western (Shreveport, LA). "A Fugitive Slave Captured." October 18, 1854.

Stukin, Stacie. "Unraveling the Myth of Quilts and the Underground Railroad." *TIME*, April 3, 2007.

Sunbury (PA) American. "A Slave Case in Cleveland." June 21, 1851.

Swetye, Cris. "Did Local Historians Research Accurately?" *Yesteryears, the Salem (OH) News*, January 26, 1993.

Taylor, Troy. "Debunking the 'History' of the Myrtles Plantation." *American Hauntings Ink* (blog). https://troytaylorbooks.blogspot.com.

Tennessean (Nashville). "A Hoax. The Riot." December 23, 1844.

Times-Picayune (New Orleans, LA). "Sarah Haynes, Alias Mielke vs. Forno Et Al." January 14, 1853.

Union (Morgantown, WV). "More Runaways." November 12, 1858.

Urbana (OH) Citizen and Gazette. "The Piatts of Logan." July 24, 1890.

Visit Baton Rouge. "The Myrtles Plantation." https://www.visitbatonrouge.com.

Washington (D.C.) Union. "Doing Unto Others as They Should Do Unto Us." November 21, 1854.

Weekly Advertiser (Montgomery, AL). "Two Slaves Escaped." September 8, 1858.

Weekly Commercial (Wilmington, NC). "Escape of Fugitive Slaves." October 29, 1852.

Weekly Marysville (OH) Tribune. "Attempt to Kidnap—Murder." June 14, 1854.

Weekly Mississippian (Jackson). "Progress of Whiggery and Niggerology in Lorain." May 7, 1841.

West, William H. Interview by W.H. Siebert, August 11, 1894. Ohio Memory, Wilbur H. Siebert Underground Railroad Collection. https://ohiomemory.org.

Western Reserve Chronicle (Warren, OH). "The Salam [*sic*] Republican Says." January 26, 1859.

Williams, Ora. "Underground Railroad Signals." *Annals of Iowa* 27, no. 4 (Spring 1946).

Wright, Giles R. "Critique: Hidden in Plain View: The Secret Story of Quilts and the Underground Railroad." HistoricCamdenCounty.com, June 4, 2001. http://historiccamdencounty.com.

Books

Blight, David W. *Race and Reunion: The Civil War in American Memory*. Belknap Press, 2001.

Bradford, Sarah H. *Scenes in the Life of Harriet Tubman*. W.J. Moses, 1869.

Buckingham, Ebenezer. *Solomon Sturges and His Descendants*. Grafton Press, 1907.

Burroughs, John. *Riverby*. Houghton, Mifflin, 1895.

Cairnes, J.E. *The Slave Power, Its Character, Career, and Probable Designs*. Parker, Son, & Bourn, 1862.

Calarco, Tom. *The Search for the Underground Railroad in South-Central Ohio*. The History Press, 2018.

Clarke, Lewis, and Milton Clarke. *Narratives of the Sufferings of Lewis and Milton Clarke*. Bela Marsh, 1846.

Coffin, Levi. *Reminiscences of Levi Coffin*. Western Tract Society, 1876.

Coleman, J. Winston. *Slavery Times in Kentucky*. University of North Carolina Press, 1940.

Dickinson, Cornelius Evarts. *A History of Belpre, Washington County, Ohio*. Globe Printing & Binding Company, 1920.

Douglass, Frederick. *Narrative of the Life of Frederick Douglass*. Anti-Slavery Office, 1845.

Drew, Benjamin. *A North-Side View of Slavery*. John P. Jewett and Company, 1856.

———. *The Refugee: Or the Narratives of Fugitive Slaves in Canada*. John P. Jewett, 1856.

Evans, Nelson Wiley. *A History of Adams County, Ohio: From Its Earliest Settlement to the Present*. E.B. Stivers, 1900.

Fleming, Thomas. *A Disease of the Public Mind: A New Understanding of Why We Found the Civil War*. Da Capo Press, 2013.

Gara, Larry. *The Liberty Line: The Legend of the Underground Railroad*. University Press of Kentucky, 1961.

Goldfield, David. *America Aflame: How the Civil War Created a Nation*. Bloomsbury Press, 2011.

Grieve, Charles Theodore. *Centennial History of Cincinnati*. Biographical Publishing Company, 1904.

Griffler, Keith P. *Front Line of Freedom*. University Press of Kentucky, 2004.

Hagedorn, Ann. *Beyond the River*. 2008. Simon & Schuster, 2004.

Harrold, Stanley. *Border War*. University of North Carolina Press, 2010.

Hise, Daniel H. *A Diary of the Life of Daniel Howell Hise From the Year 1846 to 1878*. The Salem Historical Society & the Salem Public Library, 2001.

History of Geauga and Lake Counties, Ohio. Williams Brothers, 1878.

Howe, Henry. *Historical Collections of Ohio*. Vol. 2. C.J. Krehbiel, 1902.

King, Rufus. *Ohio: First Fruits of the Ordinance of 1787*. Houghton, Mifflin, 1896.

Knepp, Gary L. *Freedom's Struggle: A Response to Slavery from the Ohio Borderlands*. Little Miami, 2008.

Larson, Kate Clifford. *Bound for the Promised Land*. Ballantine Books, 2004.

May, Samuel. *The Fugitive Slave Law and Its Victims*. American Anti-Slavery Society, 1861.

Meyers, David, and Elise Meyers Walker. *Historic Black Settlements of Ohio*. The History Press, 2020.

———. *The Reverse Underground Railroad in Ohio*. The History Press, 2022.

Middleton, Stephen. *The Black Laws*. Ohio University Press, 2005.

Mitchell, W.M. *The Under-Ground Railroad*. Richard Priddy, 1860.

Parker, John P. *His Promised Land: The Autobiography of John P. Parker, Former Slave and Conductor on the Underground Railroad*. W.W. Norton, 1996.

Peeke, Hewson L. *A Standard History of Erie County, Ohio*. Vol. 1. Lewis, 1916.

Perrin, William Henry. *History of Stark County, Ohio*. Haskin & Battey, 1881.

Phillips, Ulrich Bonnell. *American Negro Slavery*. D. Appleton, 1918.

Pollitt, Bethany Marie. "The Antislavery Movement in Clermont County." Master's thesis, Wright State University, 2012.

Randolph, W.M. *Reports of Cases Argued and Determined in the Supreme Court of Louisiana*. Vol. 8. Office of the Louisiana Courier, 1854.

Shane, Scott. *Flee North*. Celadon Books, 2023.

Siebert, Wilbur H. *Mysteries of Ohio's Underground Railroad*. Long's College Book Company, 1951.

———. *The Underground Railroad from Slavery to Freedom*. MacMillan, 1898.

Smith, William Henry. *A Political History of Slavery*. G.P. Putnam's Sons, 1903.

Snodgrass, Mary Ellen. *The Underground Railroad: An Encyclopedia of People, Places, and Operations*. M.E. Sharpe, 2008.

Trowbridge, John Townsend. *The Ferry Boy and the Financier*. Walker, Wise, 1864.

Troy, William. *Hair-Breadth Escapes From Slavery to Freedom*. Guardian Steam-Printing Offices, 1861.

Ward, Andrew. *Dark Midnight When I Rise: The Story of the Fisk Jubilee Singers*. Amstead Press, 2001.

Whinnery, Dr. John Carroll. Interviewed by W.H. Siebert, Salem, Ohio, August 21, 1892.

Williams, Byron. *History of Clermont and Brown Counties, Ohio*. Self-published, 1907.

INDEX

Washington County,
  Ohio 70, 80
Washington Courthouse,
  Ohio 121
Washington, D.C. 21
Washington, George 23,
  69, 70
Washington, Martha 23
Wayne County, Ohio
  127
Waynesville, Ohio 111
Webster, Daniel 38
Weimer, Lewis F. 91
Weller, Sam 20
Wells, Randal S. 80
Wellsville, Ohio 76
Westerville, Ohio 114
West Jefferson, Ohio 33
West Liberty, West
  Virginia 59
West Virginia 146
West, William H. 67
Wheeling, West Virginia
  58, 59, 63
Whipple, Levi 37
White, George L. 134
White, Robert 94
Wigglesworth, Fanny
  62
Wigglesworth, Vincent
  60
Wilcox, Phineas B. 138
Williamson, Jane Smith
  25
Williamson, William 24
Williams Station, West
  Virginia 24
Williamstown, West
  Virginia 70
Willis, Brit 133
Willis. Wallace 133
Wilson, Daniel P 108
Wilson, Daniel P. 108
Wilson, Hiram 20

Winchester, Philander
  53
Withers, Thornton 142
Wixom, E.C. 22
Wood County, West
  Virginia 70, 152
Wood, Henrietta 93, 94
Wood, Reuben 62

X

Xenia, Ohio 109

Y

Young, Allen 112
Young, Elisha 33
Young, Henry 112
Young, Lewis 112

Z

Zanesville, Ohio 37, 41,
  151
Zell, John 20

ABOUT THE AUTHORS

A graduate of Miami and Ohio State Universities, David Meyers has written a number of local histories, as well as several novels and works for the stage. He was recently inducted into the Ohio Senior Citizens Hall of Fame for his contributions to local history.

Elise Meyers Walker is a graduate of Hofstra University and Ohio University. She has collaborated with her father on a dozen local histories, including *Ohio's Black Hand Syndicate*, *Lynching and Mob Violence in Ohio* and *A Murder in Amish Ohio*. Both authors are available for presentations.

Visit the authors' website at https://www.explodingstove.com or follow them on Facebook at https://www.facebook.com/explodingstove and Instagram @explodingstove.